One Hundred Views of Kīlauea Volcano

VOLUME TWO: 51 - 100 | *Paintings by Helen Chellin*

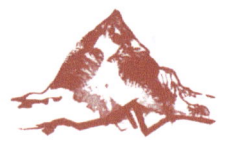

Published 2014
by Red Cinder Press

Address all inquires to:
Red Cinder Press
243 Jersey St. San Francisco, CA 94114

www.helenchellin.com

Layout Design: Carrie Ferguson

ISBN 978-0-9888875-0-3

One Hundred Views of Kīlauea Volcano

VOLUME TWO: 51 - 100 | *Paintings by Helen Chellin*

PREFACE | *One Hundred Views Of Kīlauea Volcano Volume Two: 51 – 100*

This book completes the series of paintings inspired by the volcano and the people who live and work on it. The first fifty were published last year in book format with an introduction by Christina Heliker, which is reprinted here with her permission. The first fifty paintings in this series were exhibited at the Wailoa Arts and Cultural Center in Hilo, Hawai'i in October 2013.

Helen Chellin
January 2014

Hokusai's work "One Hundred Views of Mt Fuji" is the inspiration
for this series of paintings.

This book is dedicated to him and to Christina Heliker, geologist and photographer,
and geologist Margaret T. Mangan.

"We're hanging in the de Young!" I was in my office at the summit of Kīlauea Volcano when Maggie telephoned with this surprising news. Dr. Margaret Mangan and I are volcanologists who worked together for many years at the U.S. Geological Survey's Hawaiian Volcano Observatory. Scenes from our days in the field during Kīlauea's eruption had been captured on canvas by Helen Chellin, then artist-in-residence at the de Young Museum in San Francisco.

Helen takes her inspiration from her own observations and from images that scientists record in the field. In 2006, she sought out Maggie to learn more about the USGS photographs on the Observatory website. Their meeting ultimately led to a tandem lecture at the de Young entitled "The Artist and the Geologist". I met Helen soon afterwards in Hawai'i. Over the next five years, I visited her studio whenever she was staying on the island, always eager to see her latest work. Together we hiked the shoreline at South Point and the summit of Kīlauea and shared our perceptions of the volcanic landscape. We discovered the common ground where the concerns of scientist and artist overlap. Both are mindful of color, scale, pattern, and intensity. Both want to record the forces that shaped the island.

In 2008, Helen and I accompanied Maggie to an international conference on volcanoes in Iceland. We spent a week on fieldtrips led by Icelandic volcanologists, trekking across fields of pumice and lava. At night, Helen worked on her artist's book, incorporating not only her paintings and drawings, but bits of maps and legends, pages from field guides, photographs of Icelanders, birds, and scientists.

I realized then that Helen is fascinated with connections—between culture and volcanoes and the people who strive to understand them. Her paintings rarely depict only volcanic activity, but include scientists and their instruments, birds, the trace of an earthquake, houses, historical figures, and onlookers. Her paintings tell stories.

The photographs that inspire Helen record a single moment, but in her paintings time is fluid, with scenes from Kīlauea's past blending with the present. Her paintings flow from the concrete to the abstract, conveying the mystery of this earth, which the hard facts of science can never dispel.

51 | Wind farm and Hawaiian stilts

2013
16" x 20"
acrylic paint on canvas

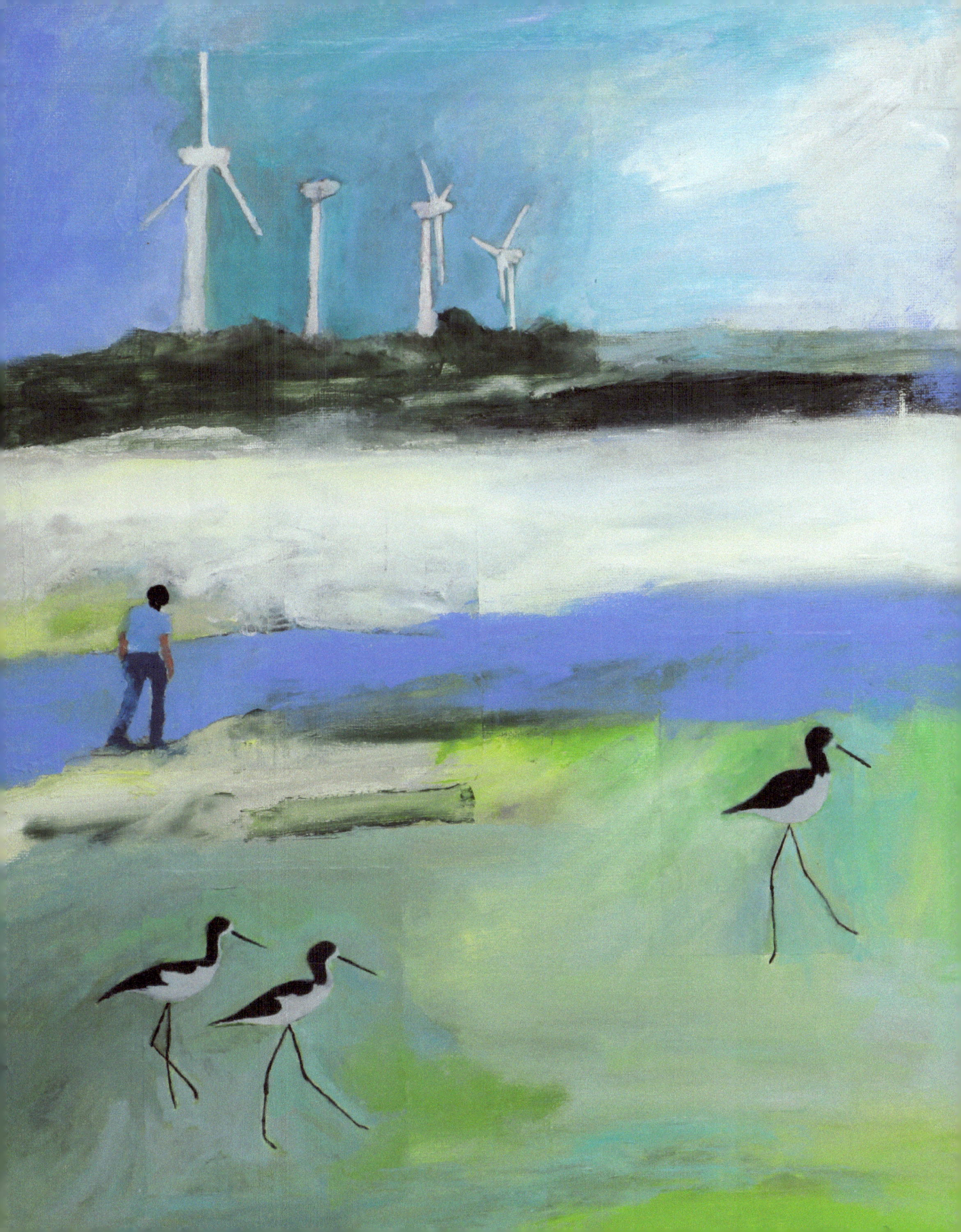

| Red bird - blue skies

2013
16"x 20"
acrylic paint on canvas

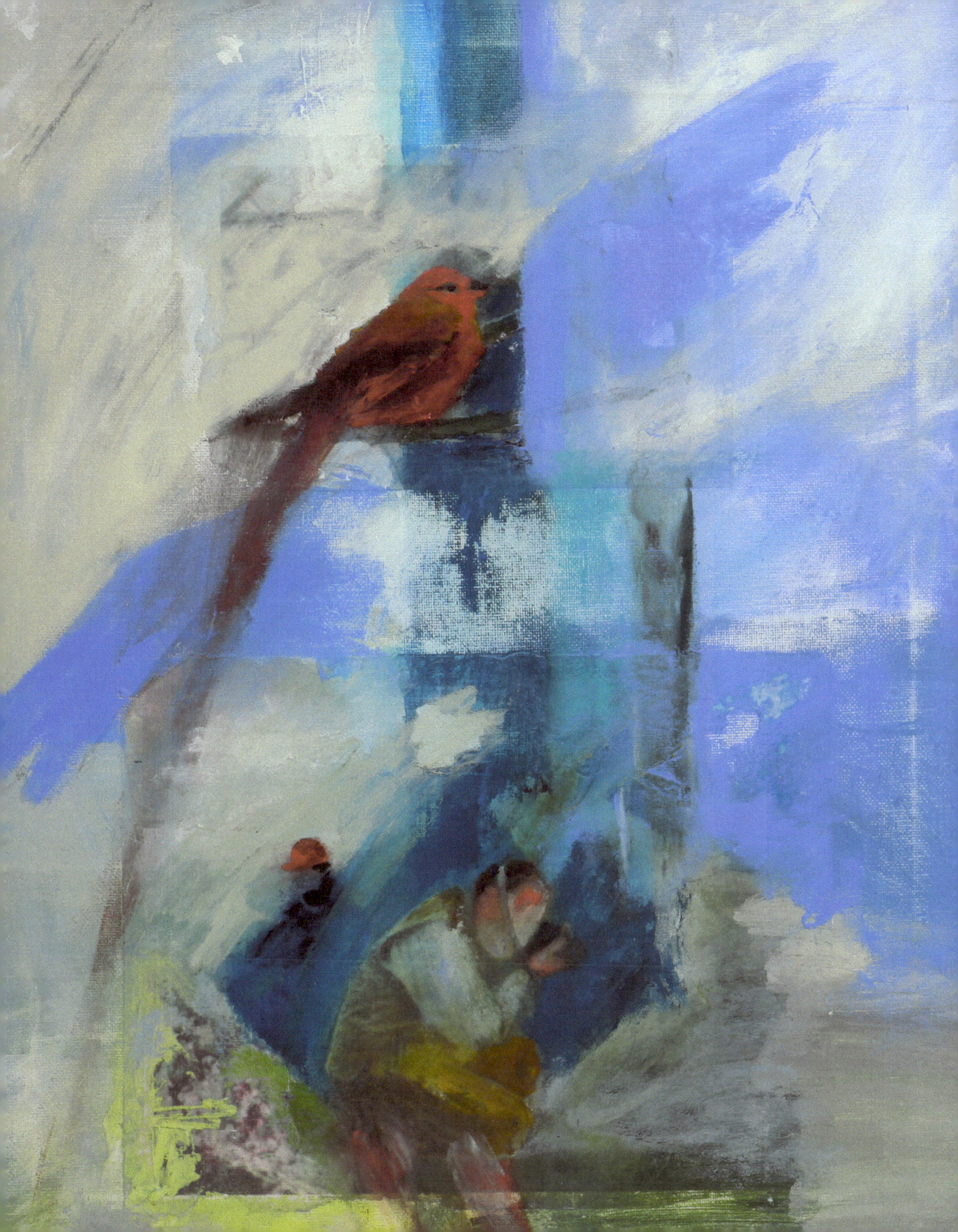

53 | Mejiro under lehua flower

2013
16"x 20"
acrylic paint on canvas

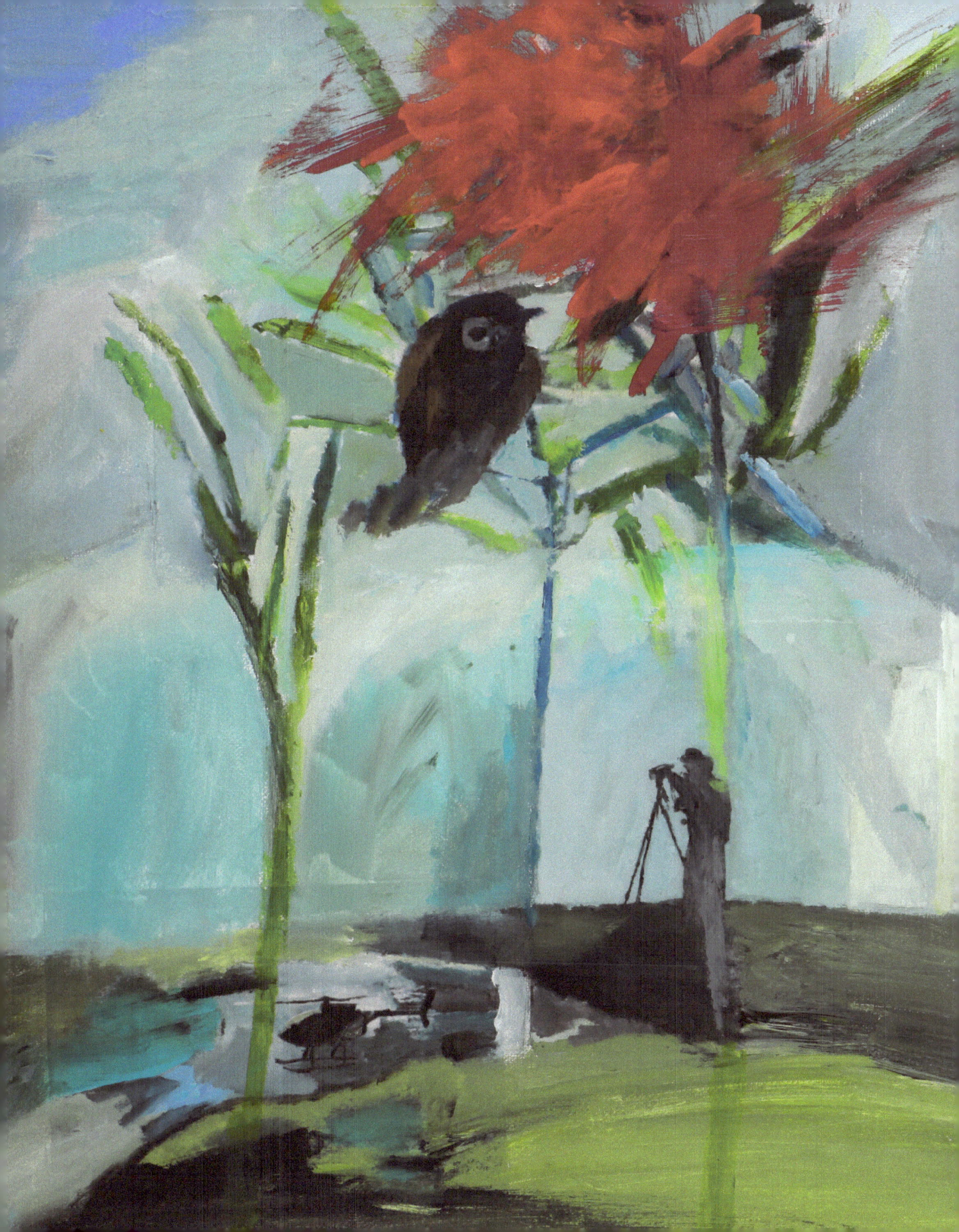

| Kīlauea oases

2013
16"x 20"
acrylic paint on canvas

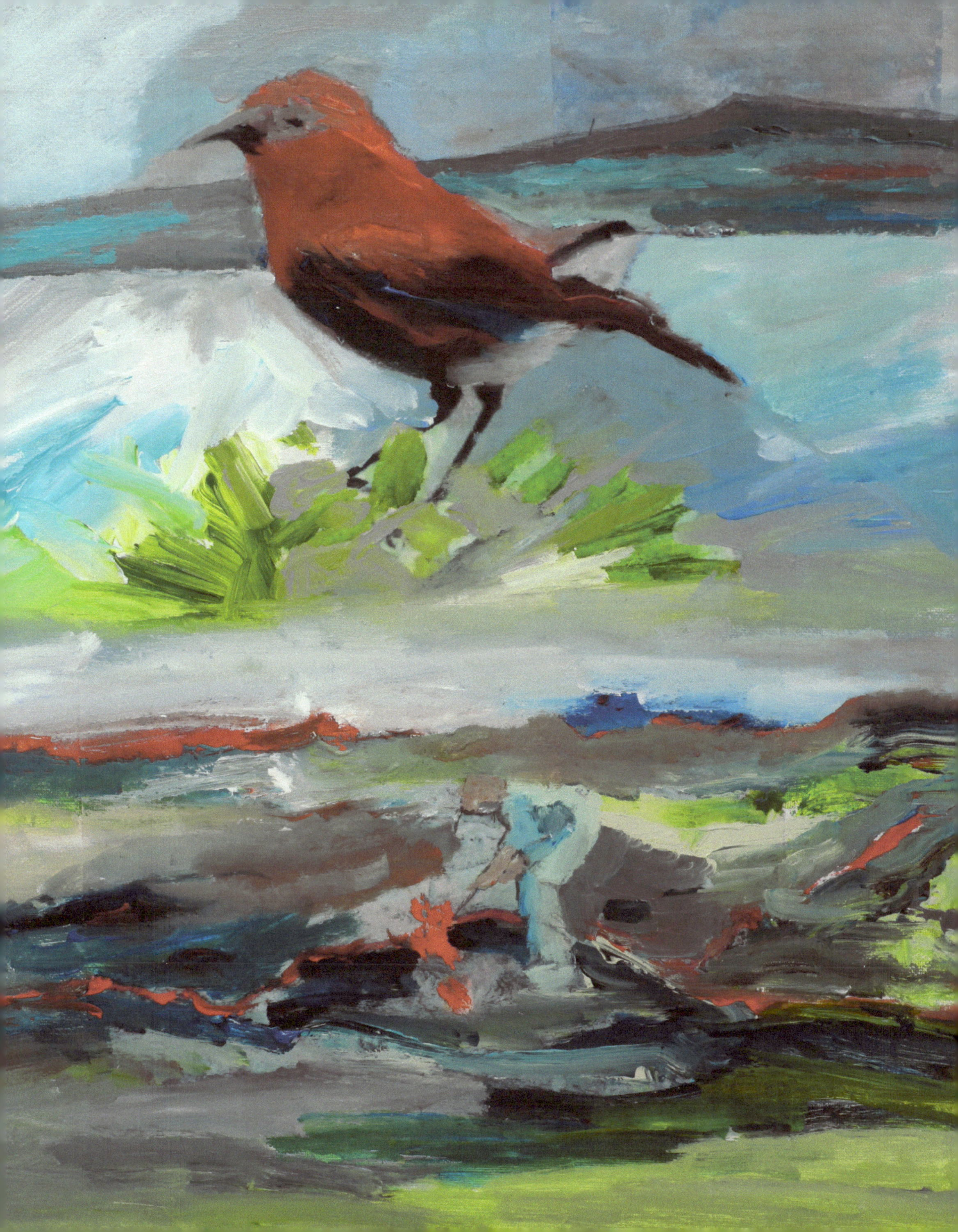

55 | # Kīlauea cat and bird

2013
16" x 20"
acrylic paint on canvas

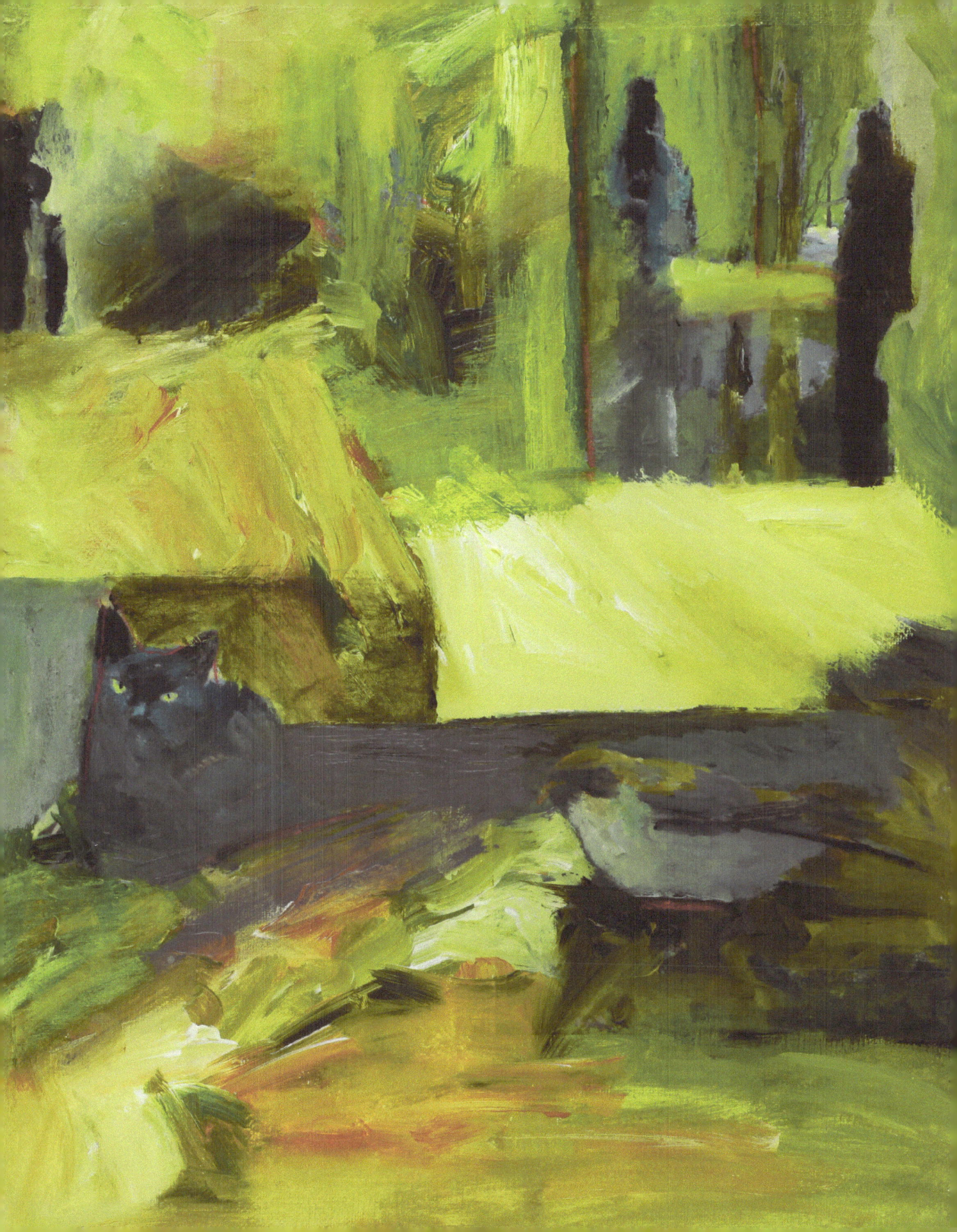

| Two black noddies over water

2013
16"x 20"
acrylic paint on canvas

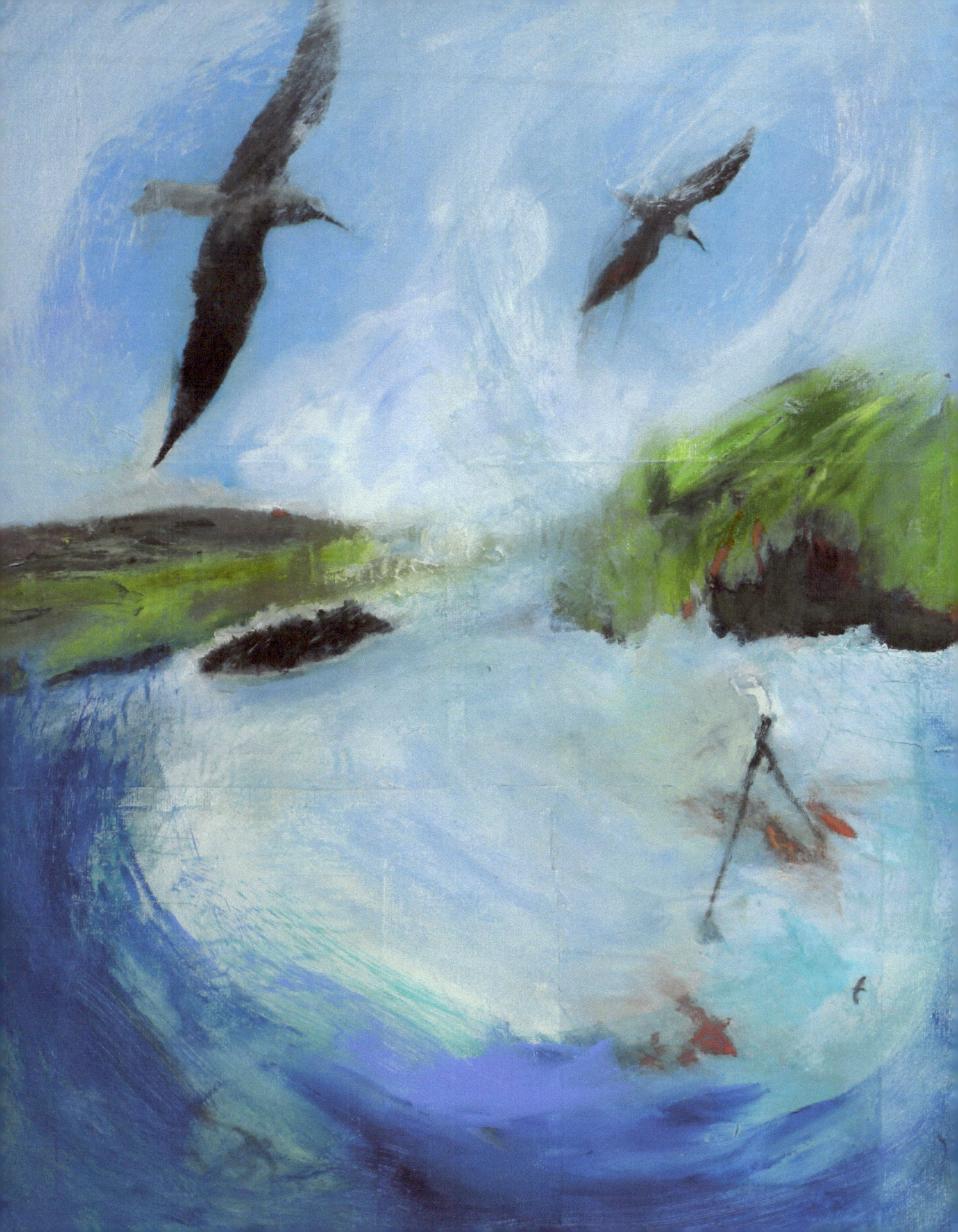

Cohabitation

2013
16"x 20"
acrylic paint on canvas

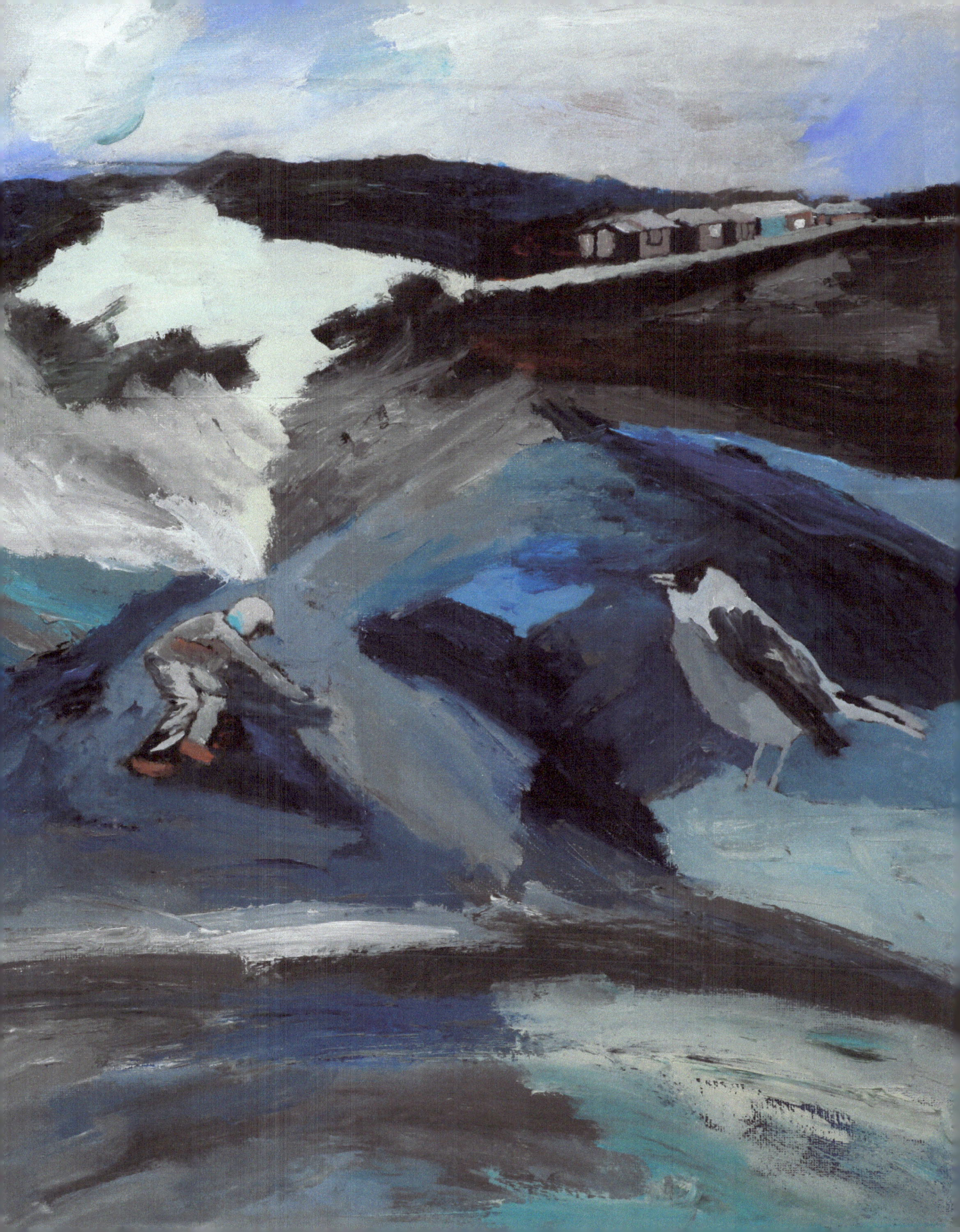

| Nēnē watching

2013
16"x 20"
acrylic paint on canvas

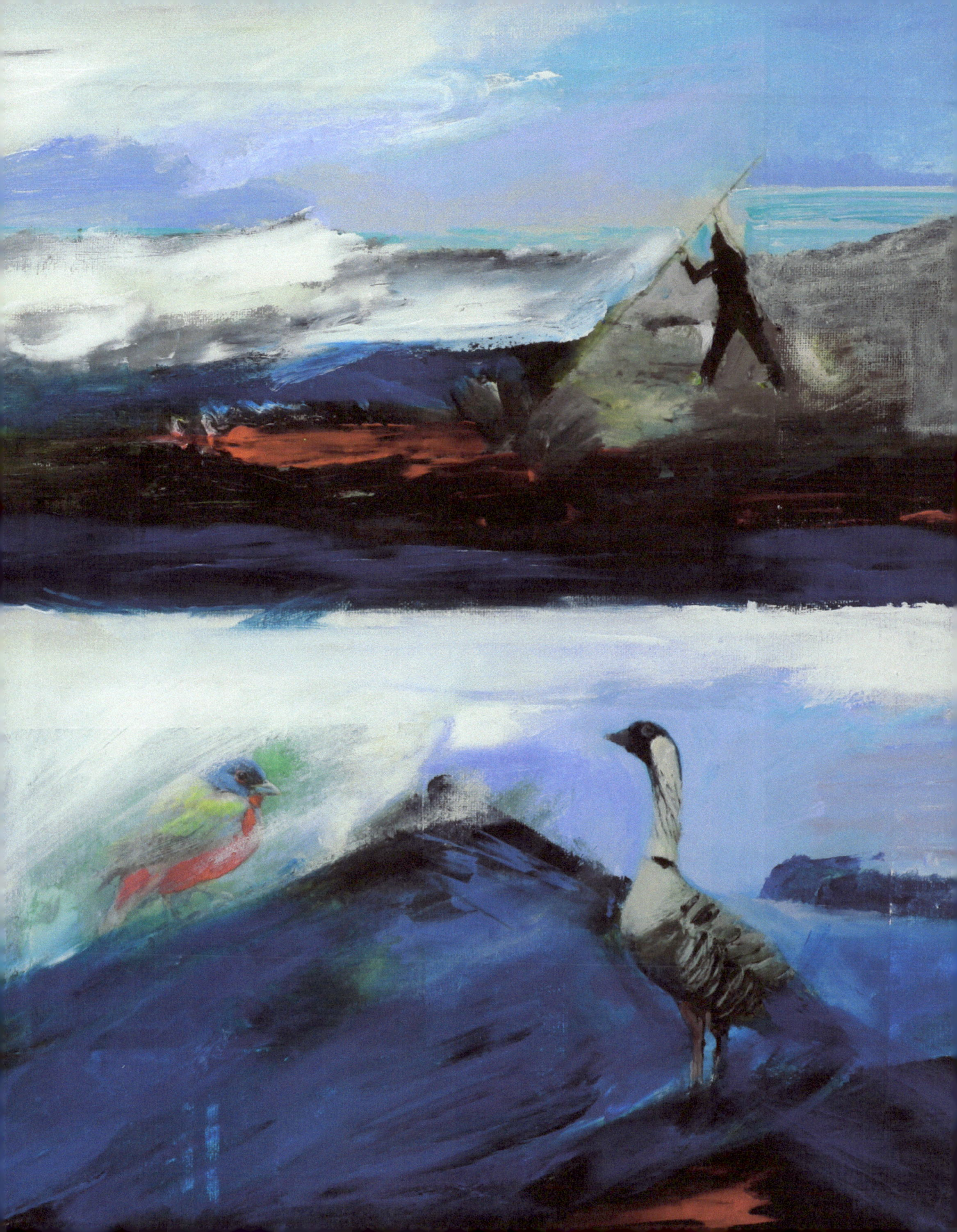

| Halemaʻumaʻu crater views

2013
16" x 20"
acrylic paint on canvas

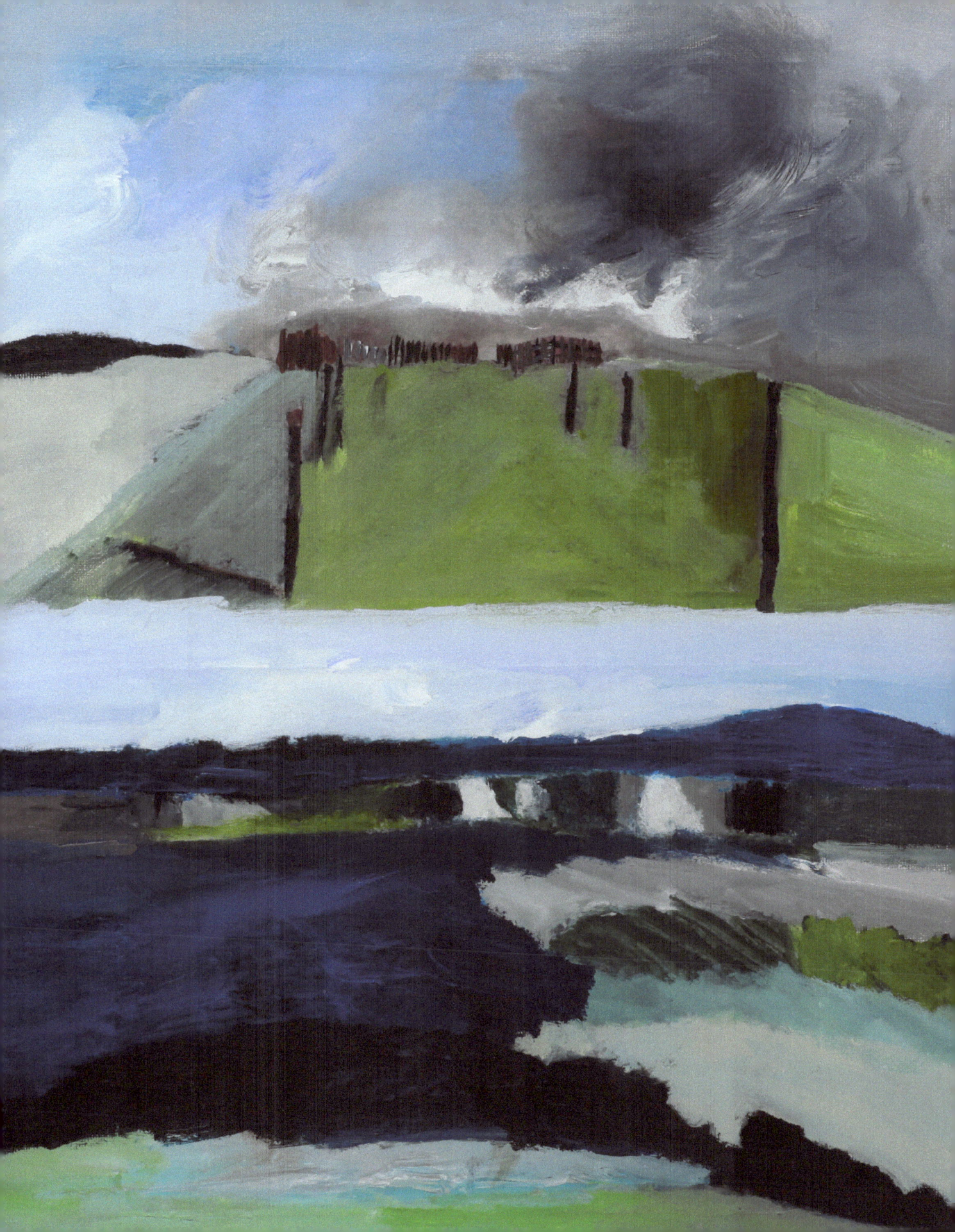

| Pairs

2013
16" x 20"
acrylic paint on canvas

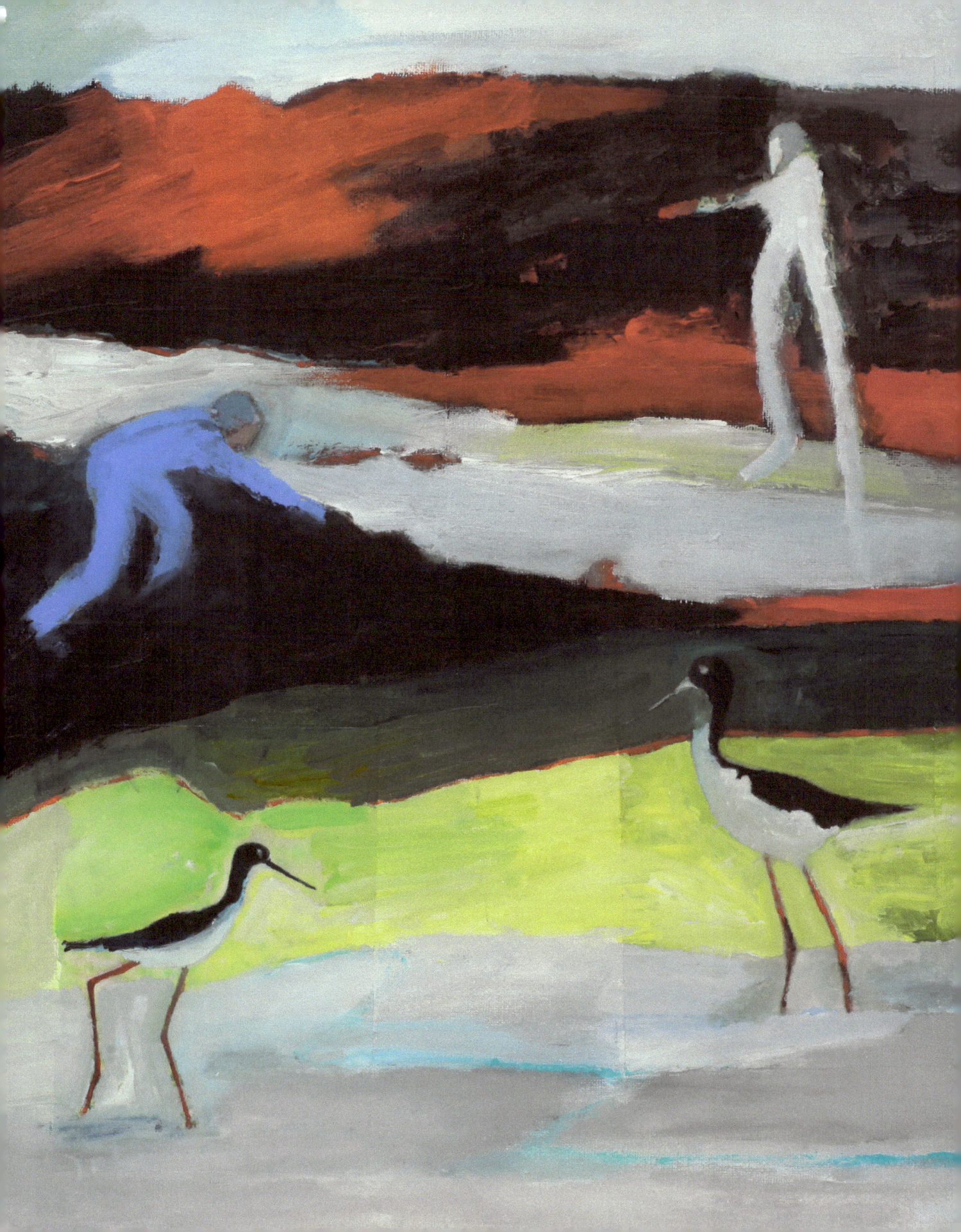

61 | Observers

2013
16"x 20"
acrylic paint on canvas

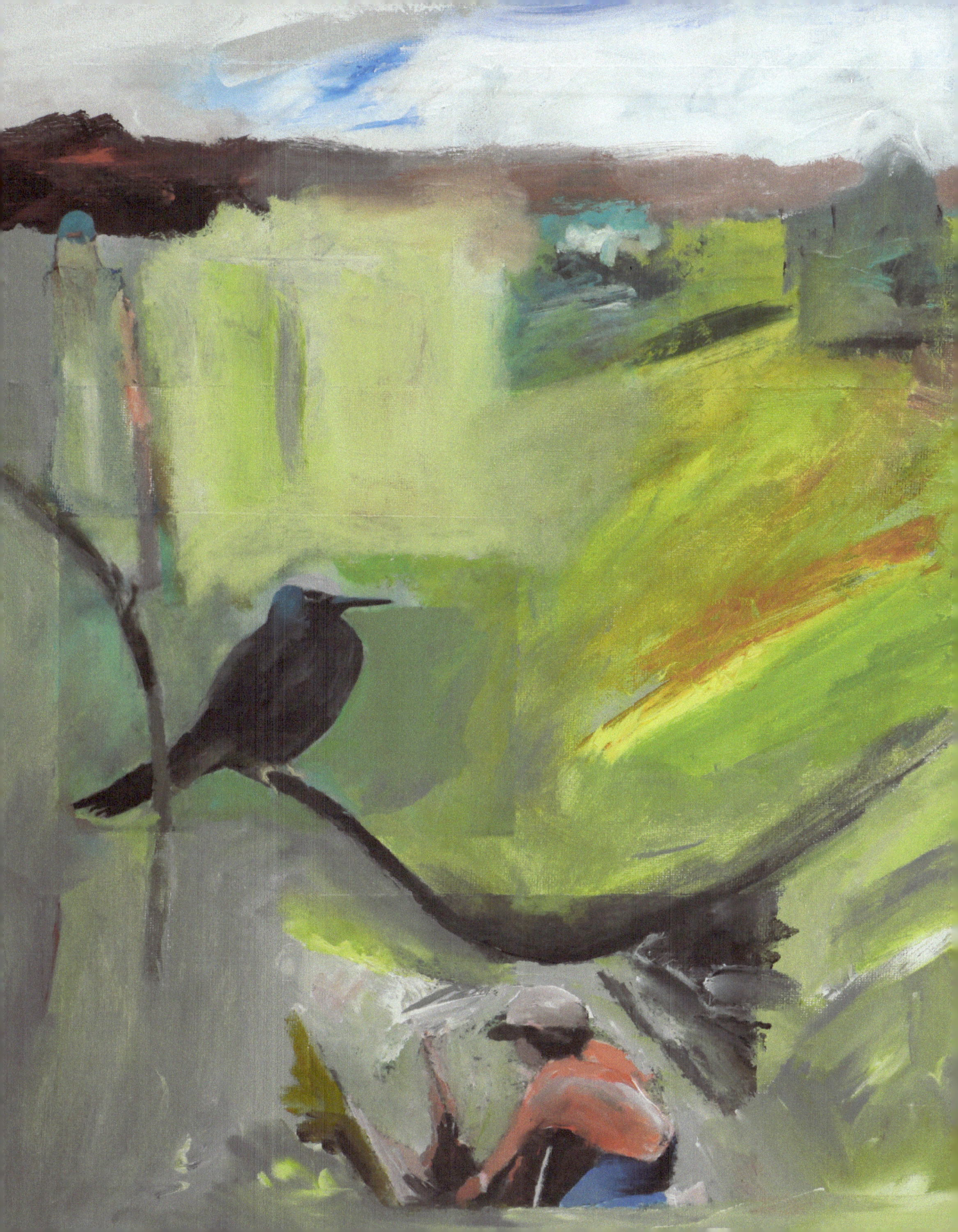

| Red bird in green fields

2013
16" x 20"
acrylic paint on canvas

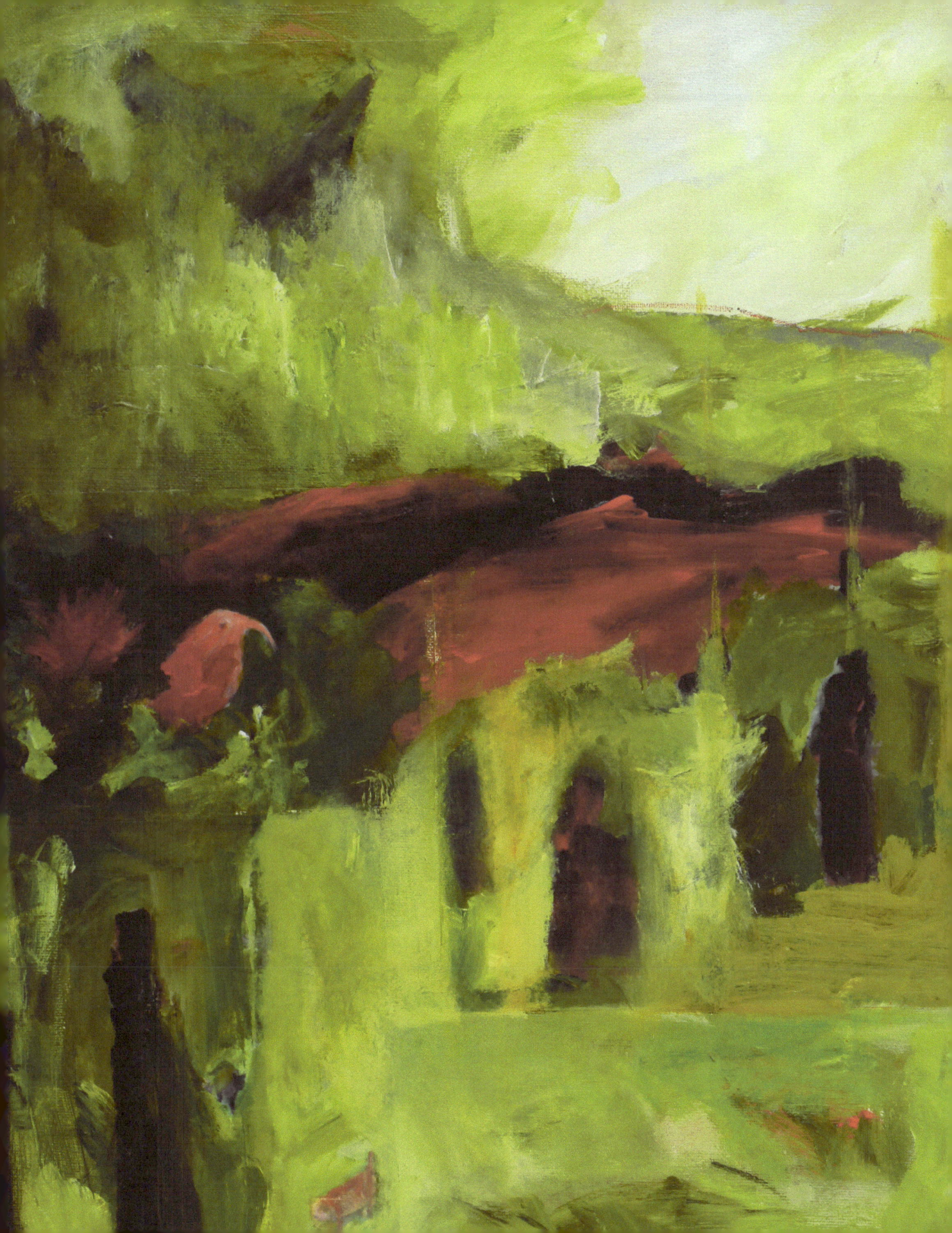

63 | Stories

2013
16"x 20"
acrylic paint on canvas

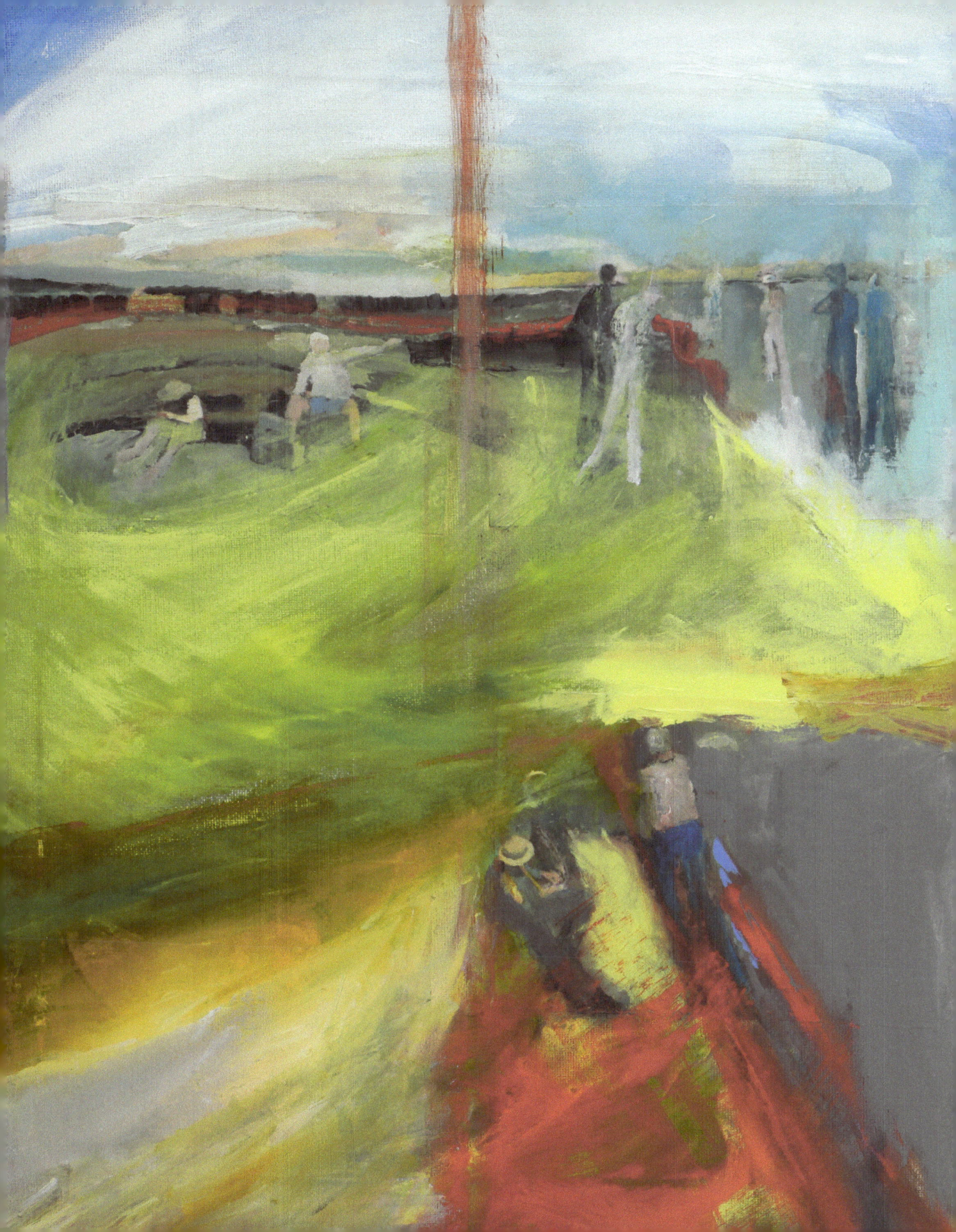

| Shifting Kīlauea

2013
16"x 20"
acrylic paint on canvas

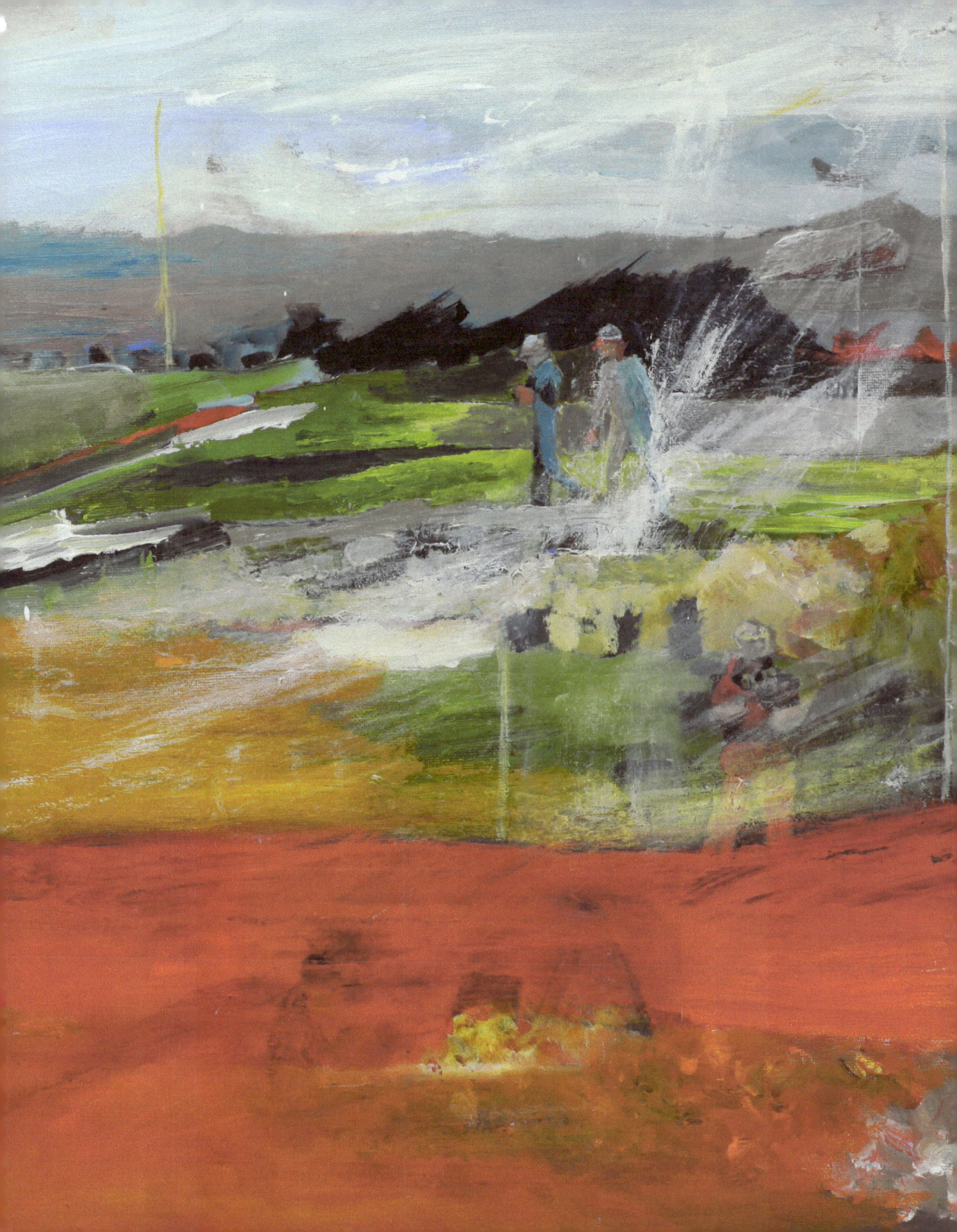

65 | Yellow and red

2013
16" x 20"
acrylic paint on canvas

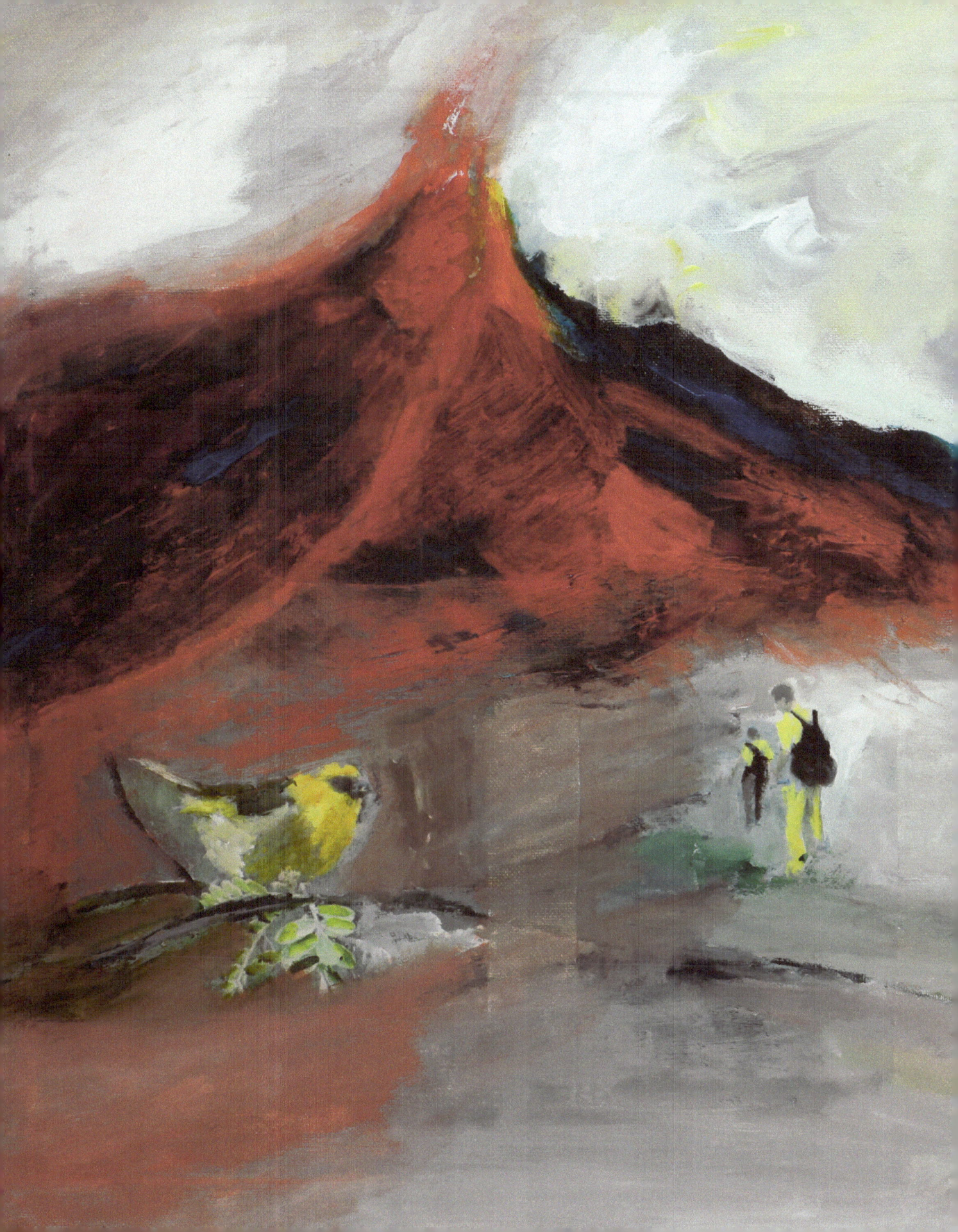

2013
16"x 20"
acrylic paint on canvas

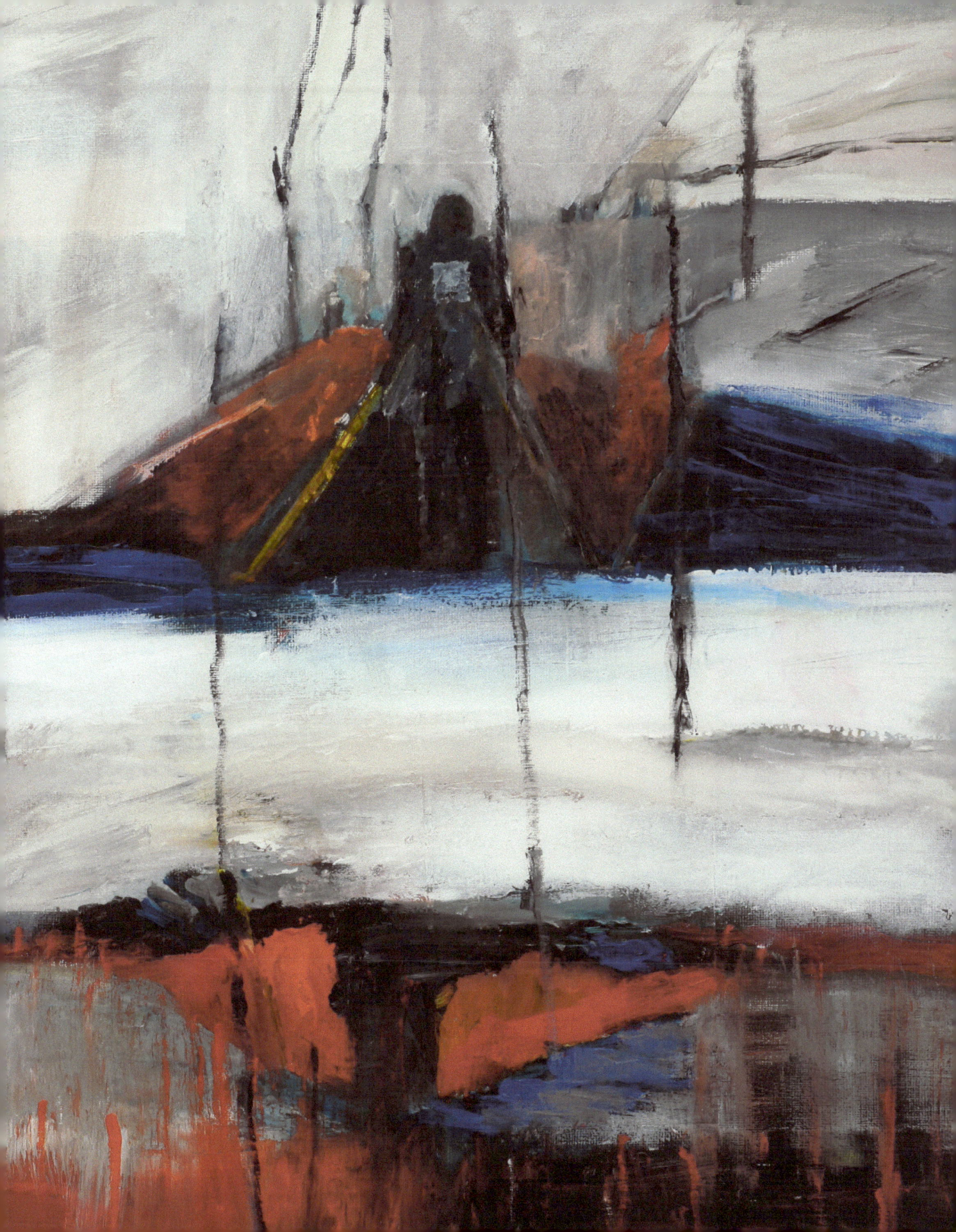

67 | Cloud cover

2013
16"x 20"
acrylic paint on canvas

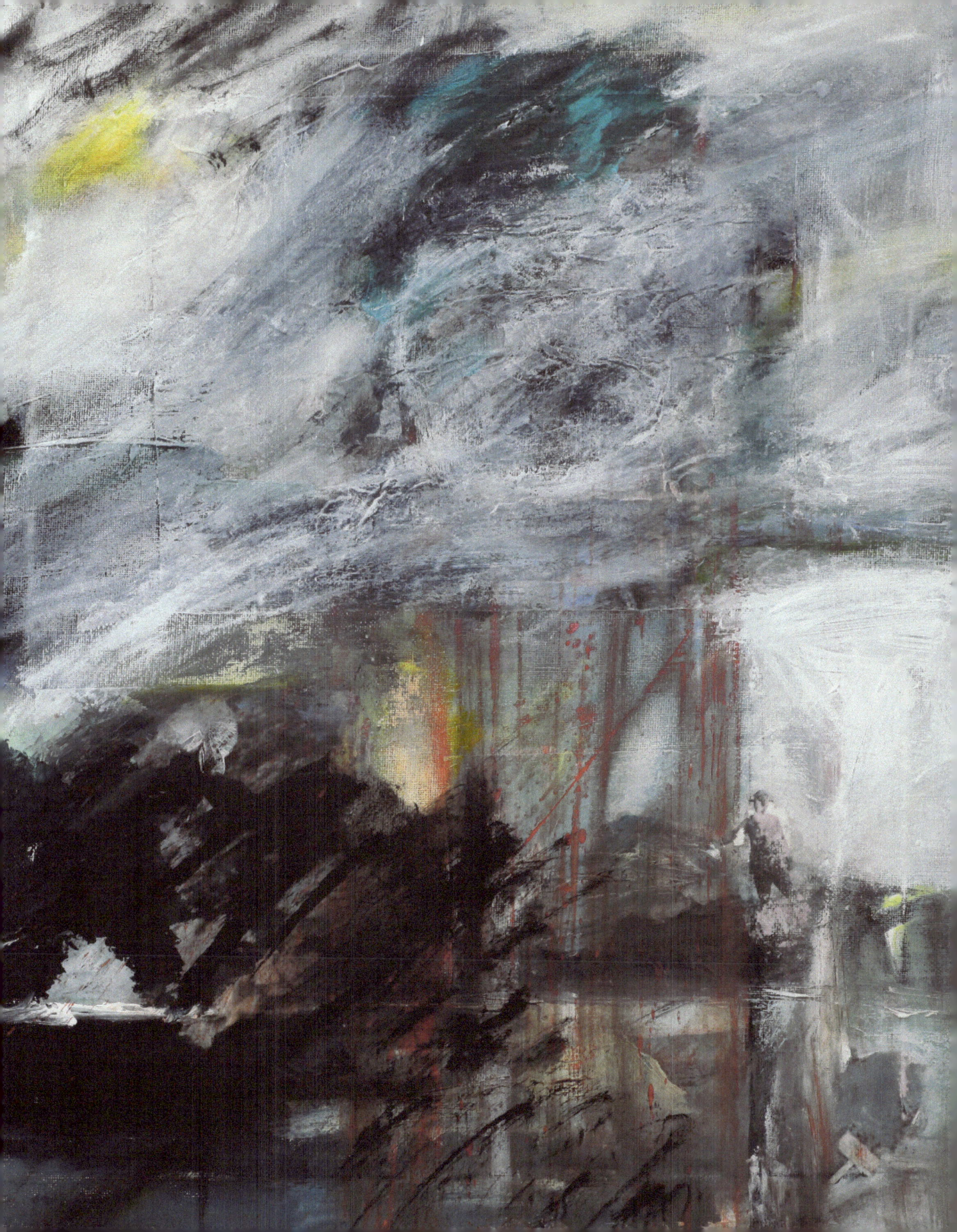

| Almost lost on lava fields

2013
16"x 20"
acrylic paint on canvas

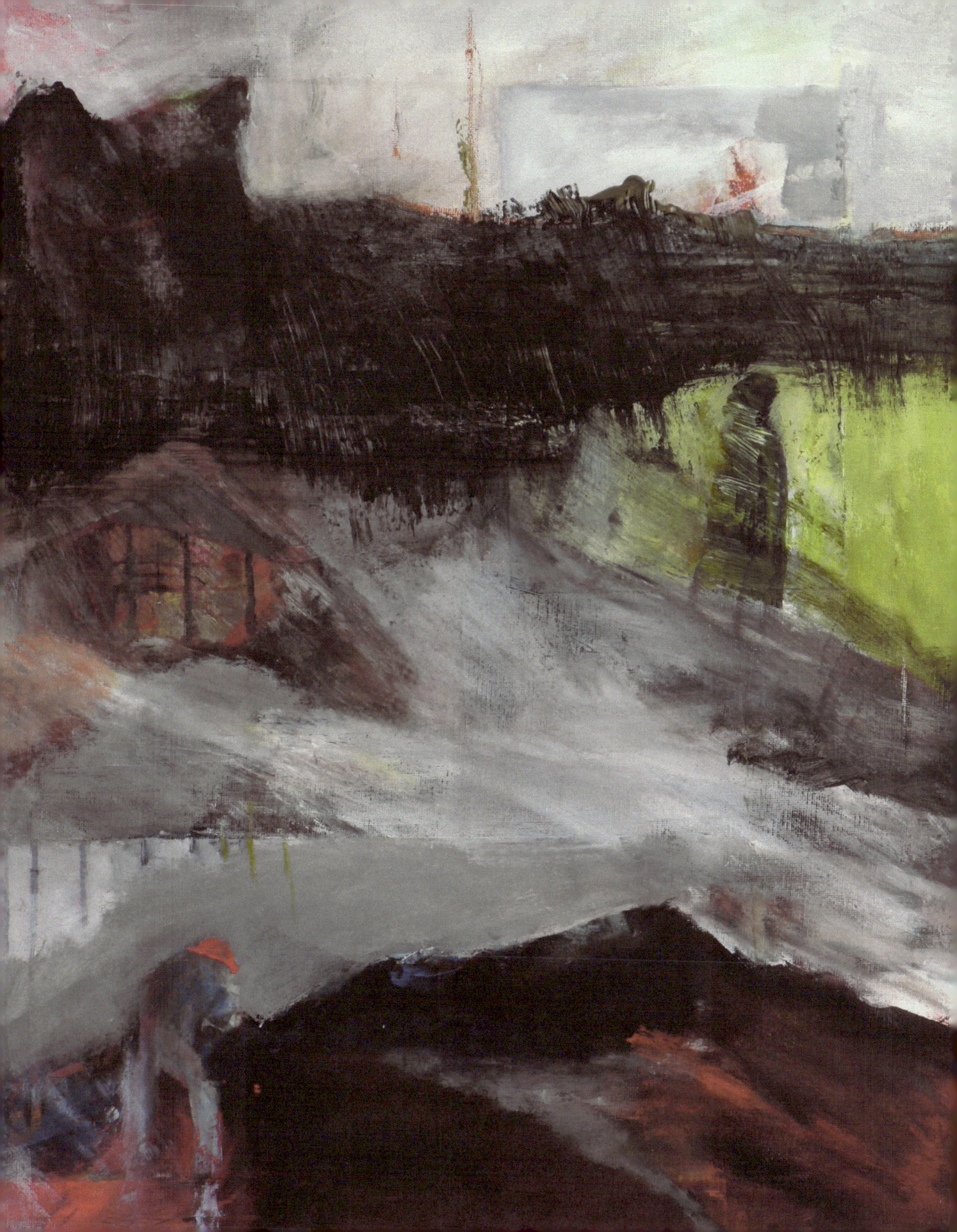

69 | Measuring lava temperatures

2013
16"x 20"
acrylic paint on canvas

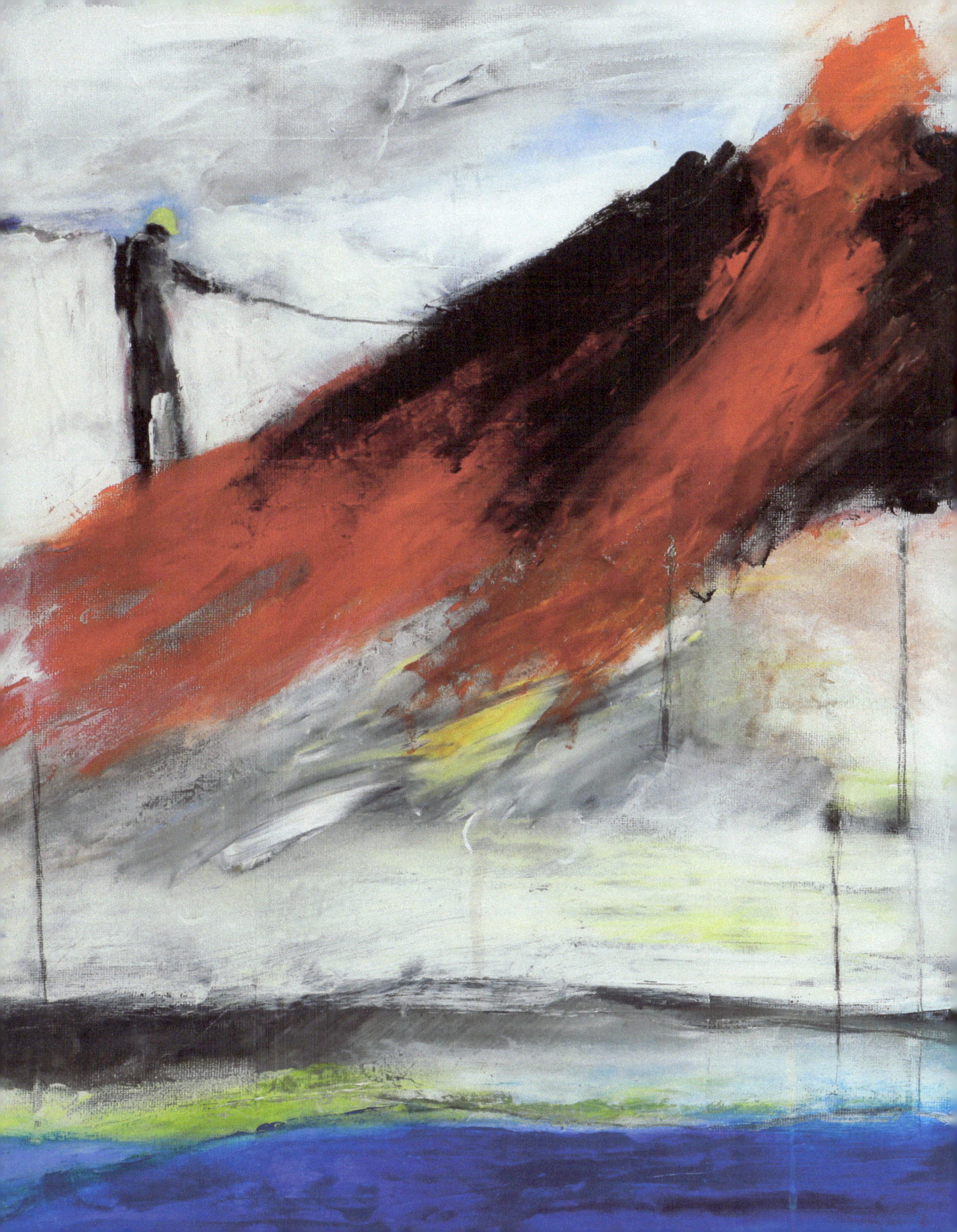

| Getting a second opinion

2013
16"x 20"
acrylic paint on canvas

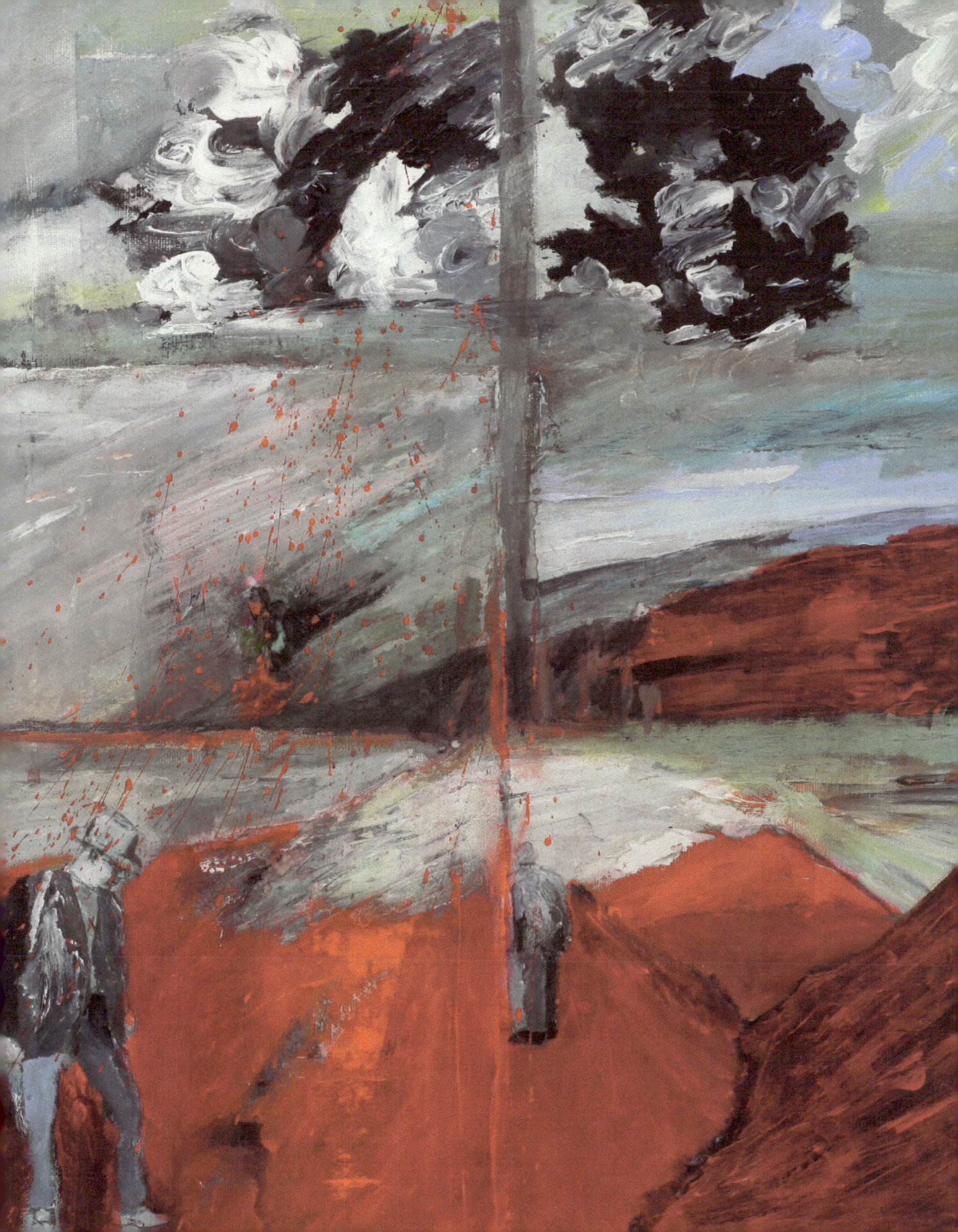

| Reds, whites, and blues

2013
16" x 20"
acrylic paint on canvas

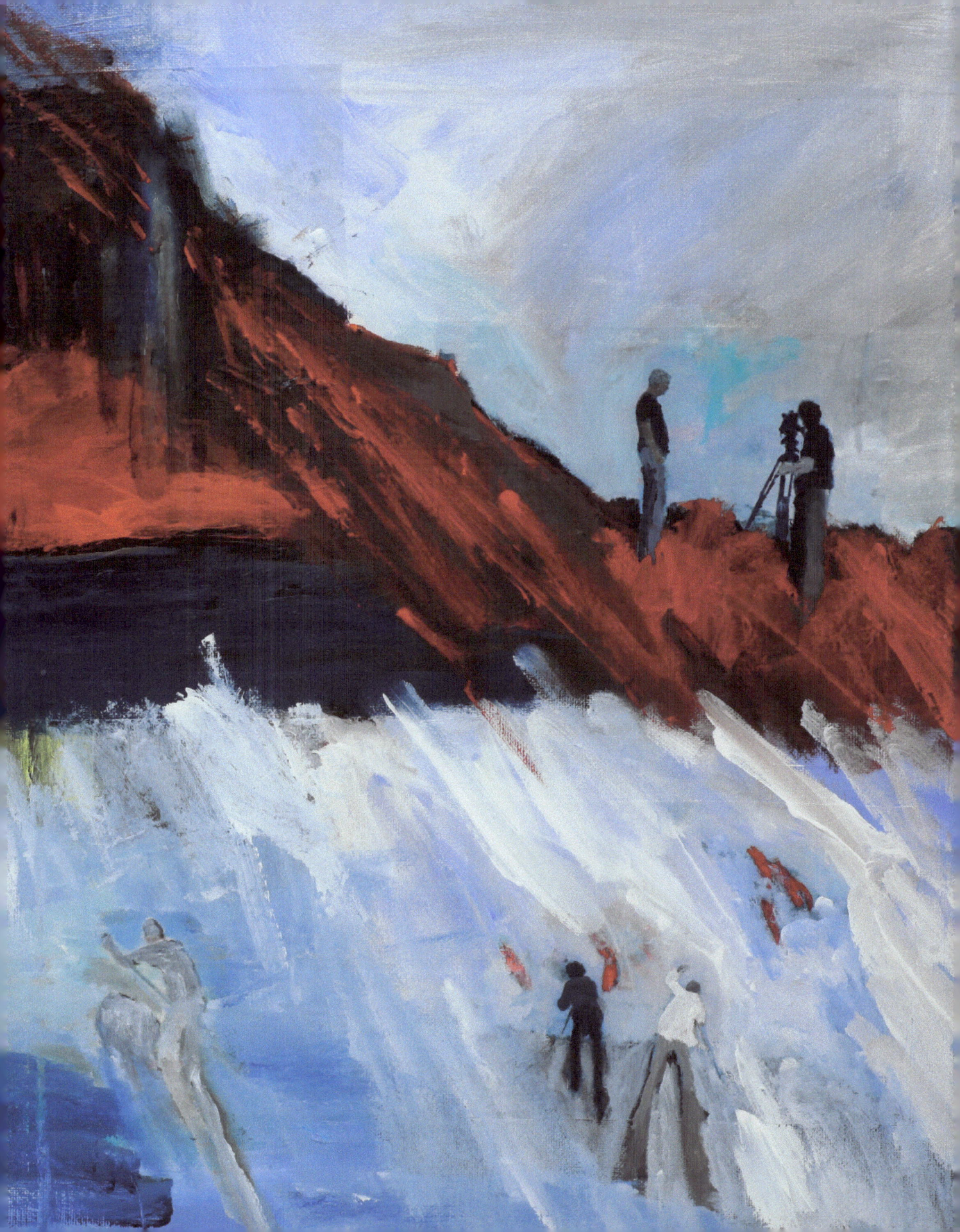

| Viewing crater

2013
16" x 20"
acrylic paint on canvas

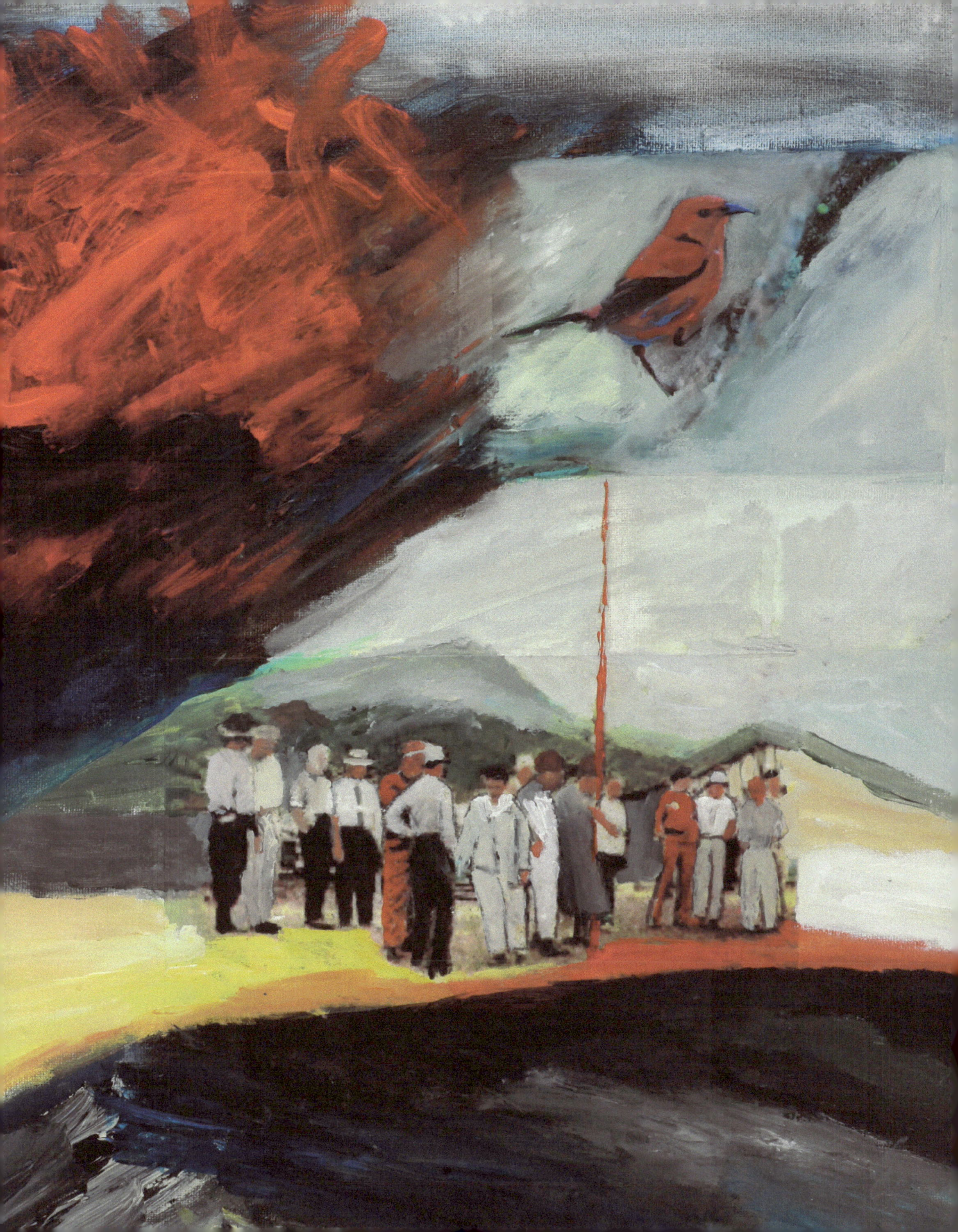

| Kīlauea geologists - fieldwork

2013
16"x 20"
acrylic paint on canvas

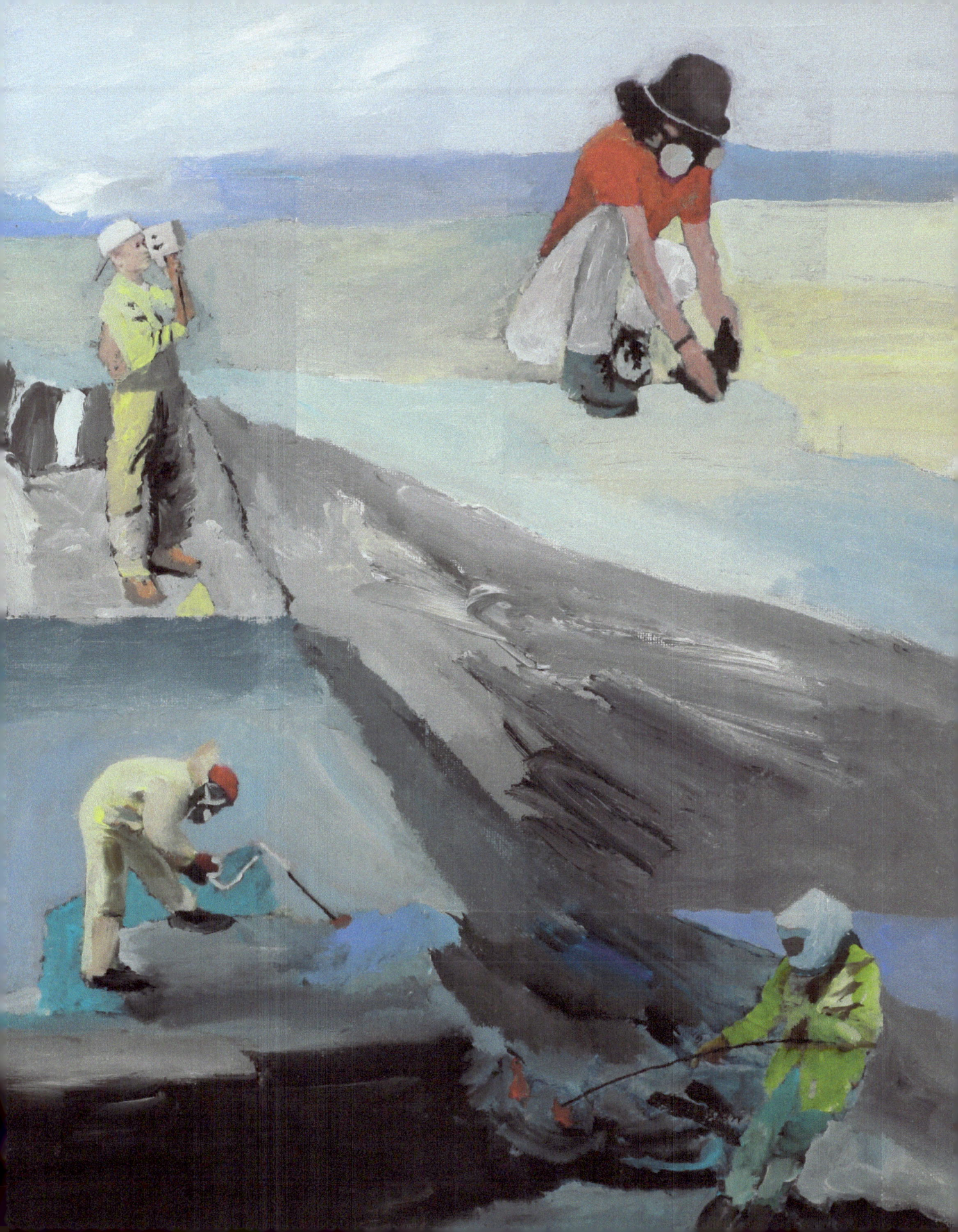

| Web cams on north side of Puʻu ʻŌʻō crater

2013
16" x 20"
acrylic paint on canvas

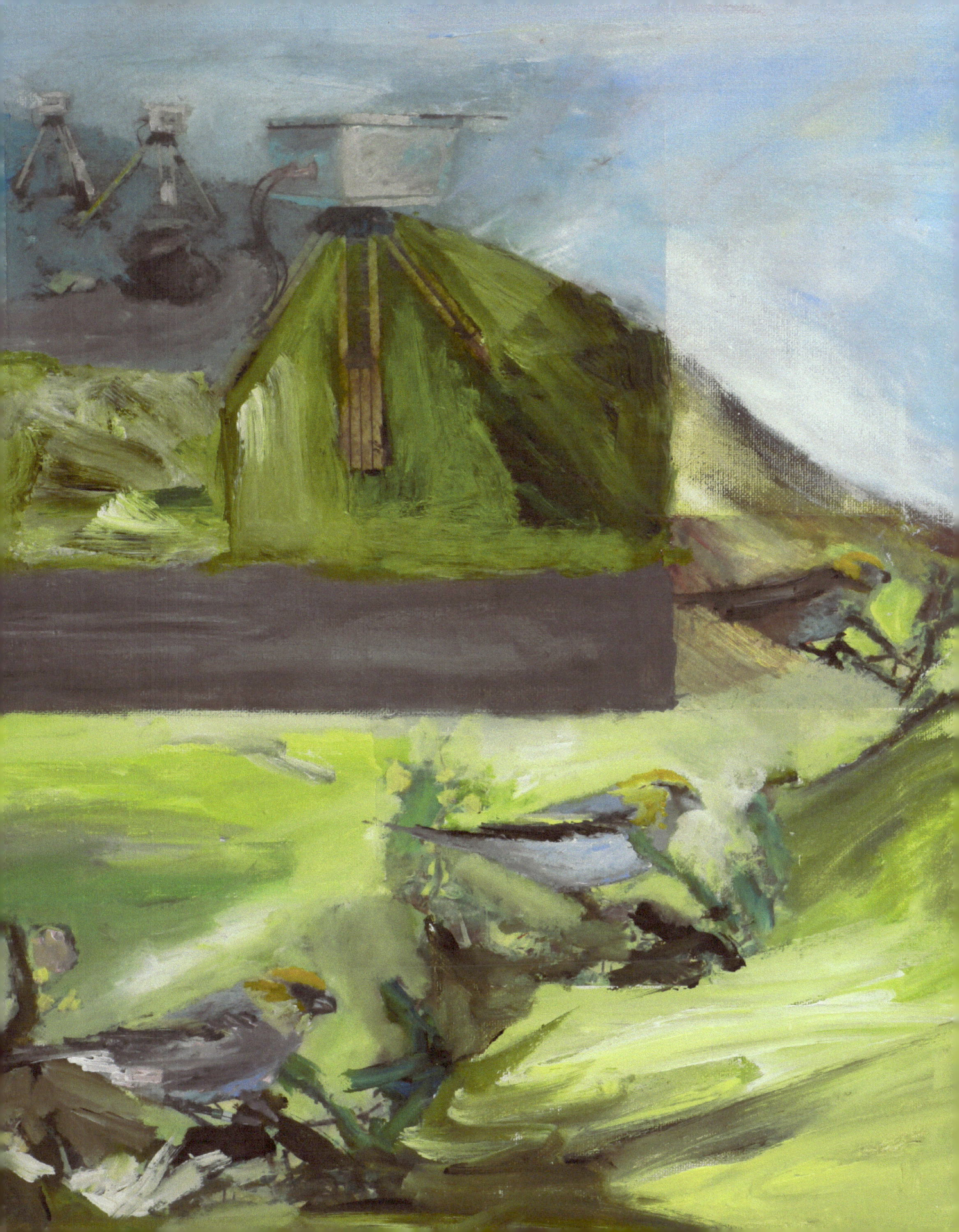

| Kalapana animal rescue

2013
16"x 20"
acrylic paint on canvas

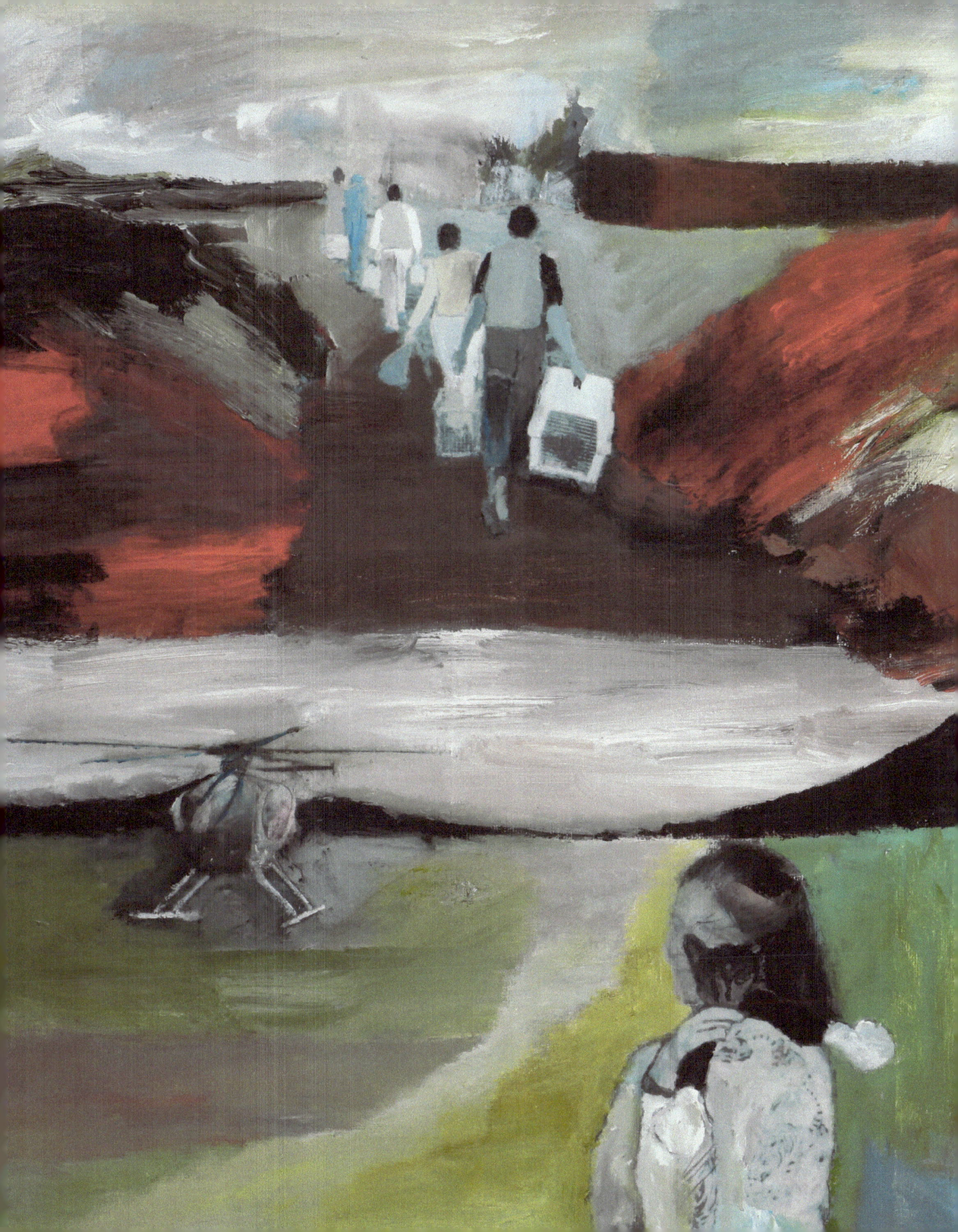

| Crossing paths

2013
16"x 20"
acrylic paint on canvas

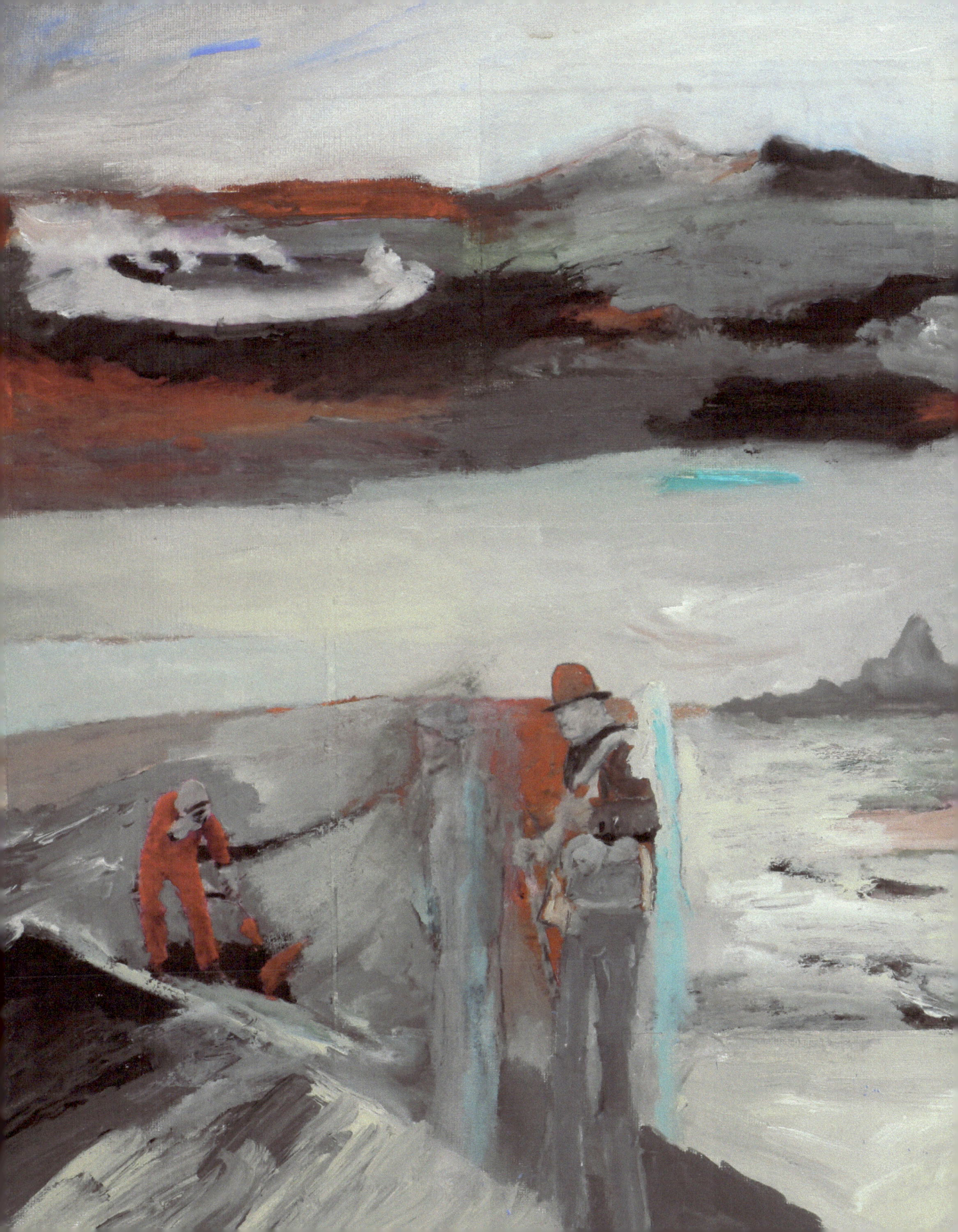

| Park visitors

2013
16"x 20"
acrylic paint on canvas

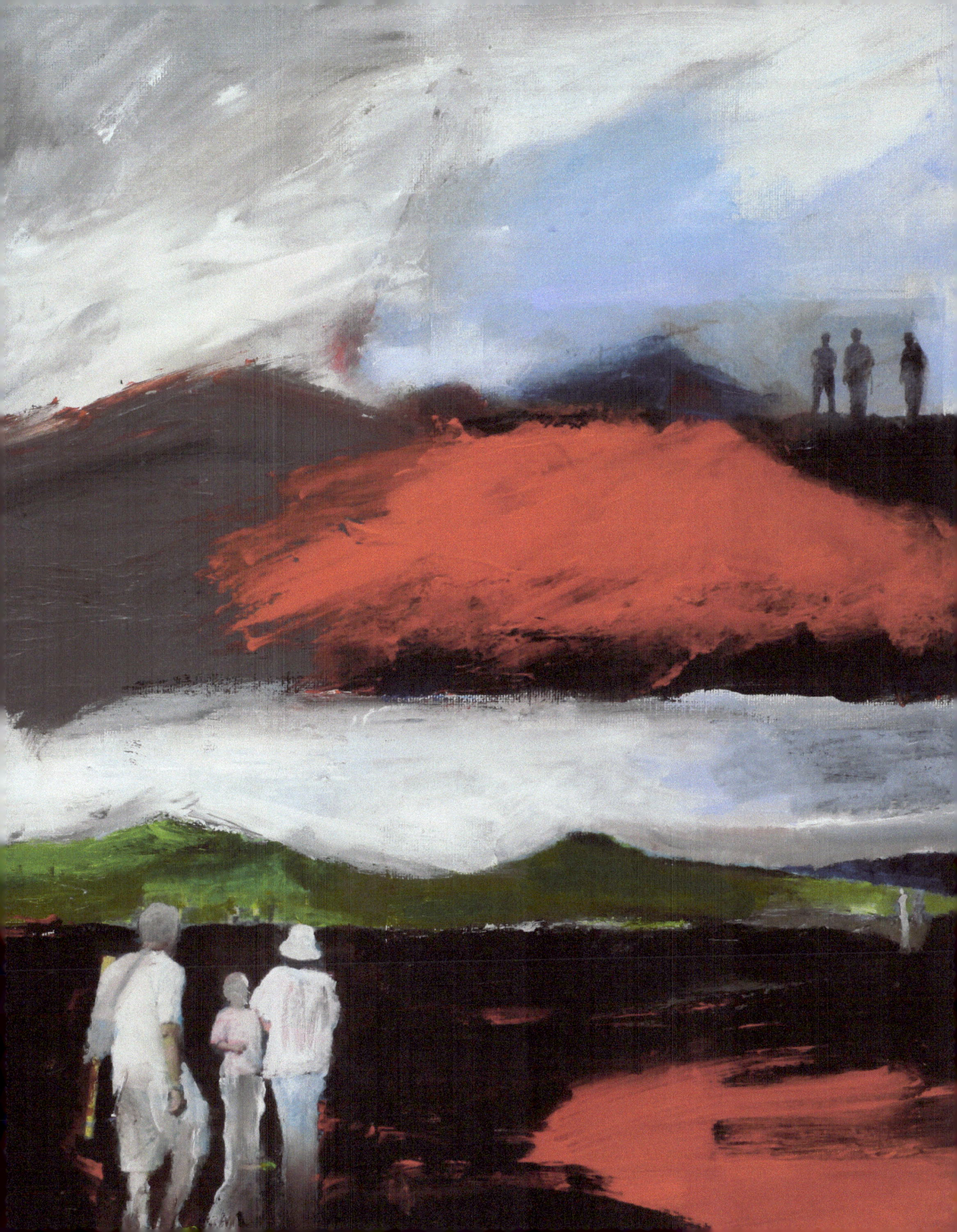

| Three at Puʻu ʻŌʻō vent

2013
16" x 20"
acrylic paint on canvas

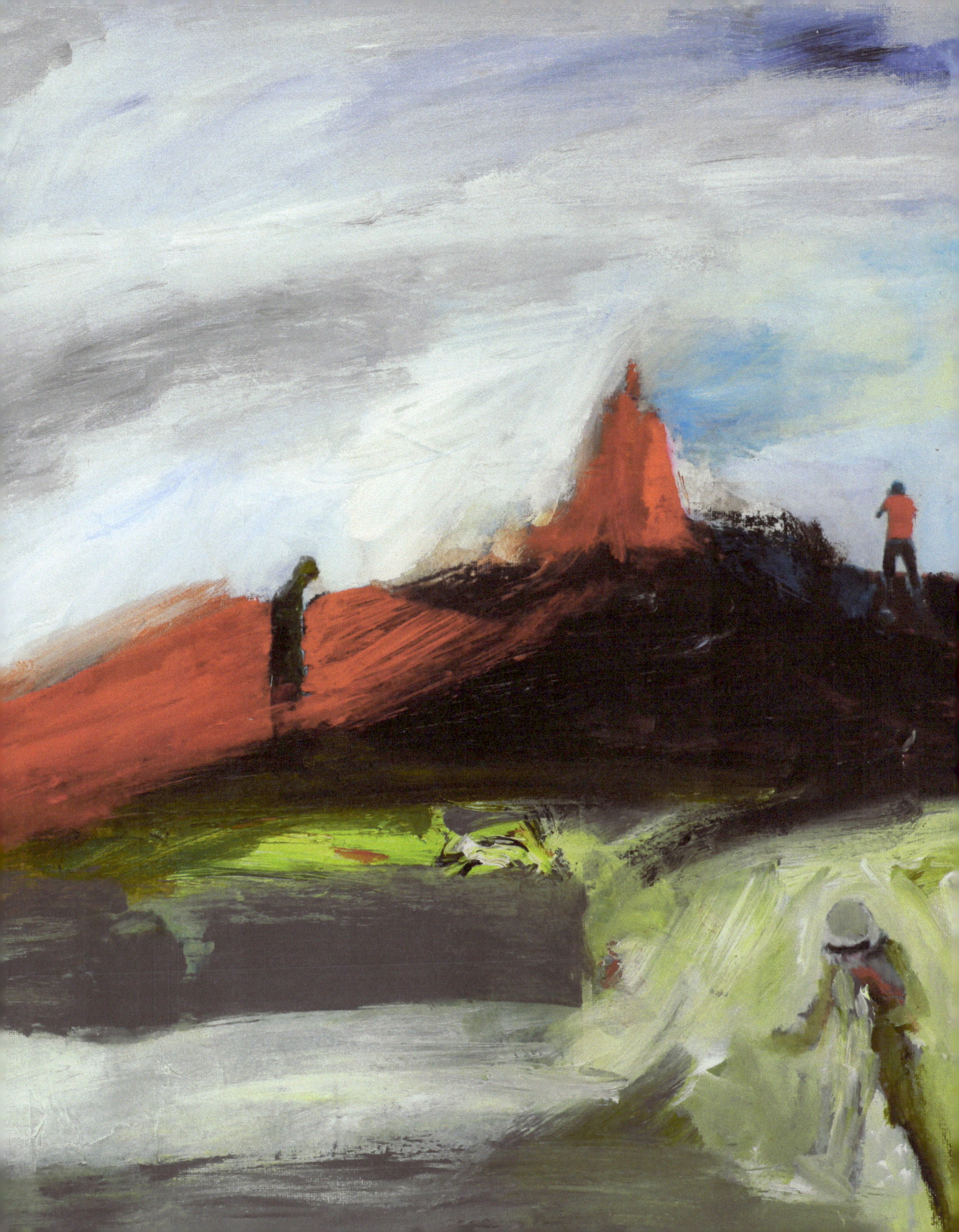

| Watching and tracking

2013
16" x 20"
acrylic paint on canvas

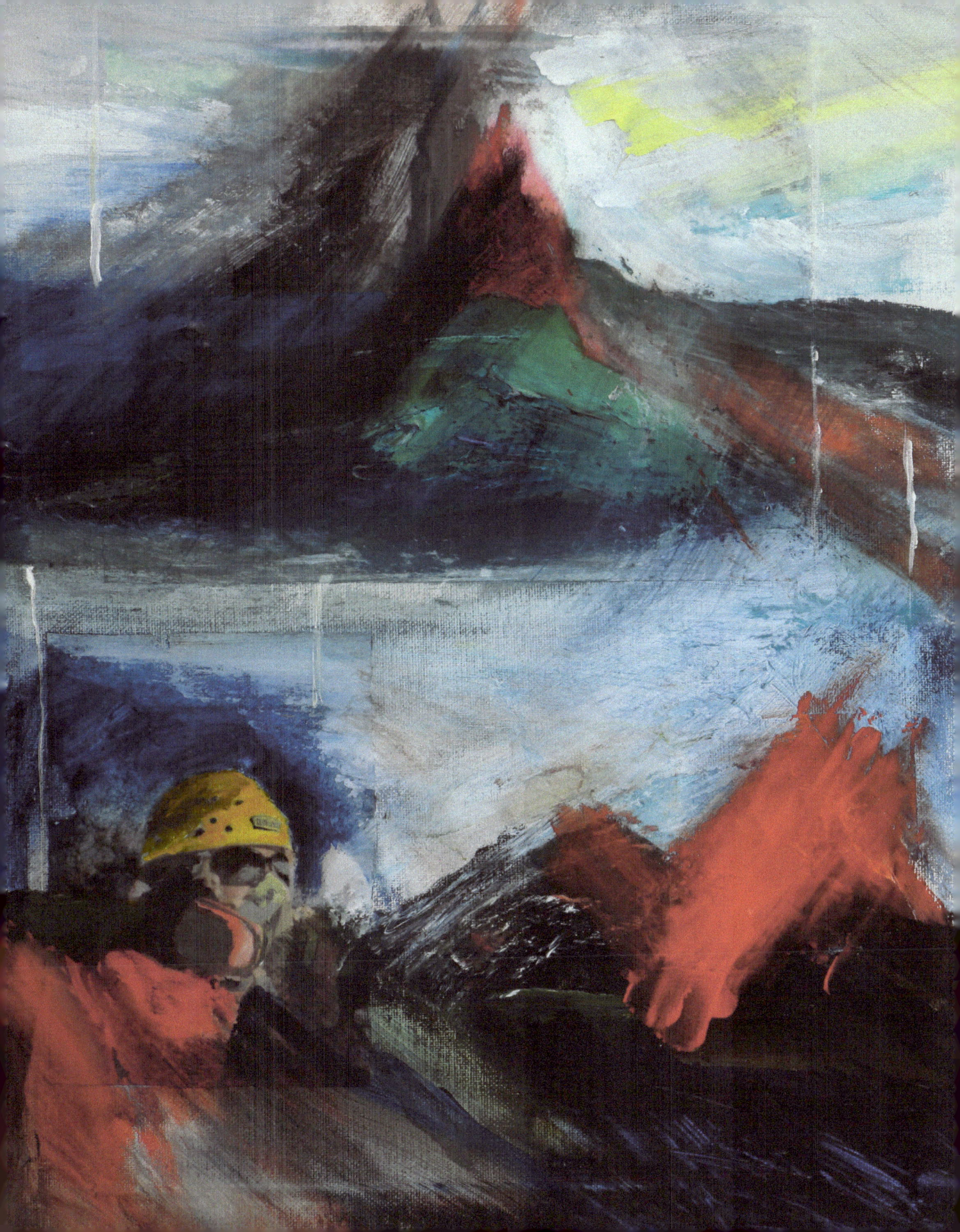

2013
16"x 20"
acrylic paint on canvas

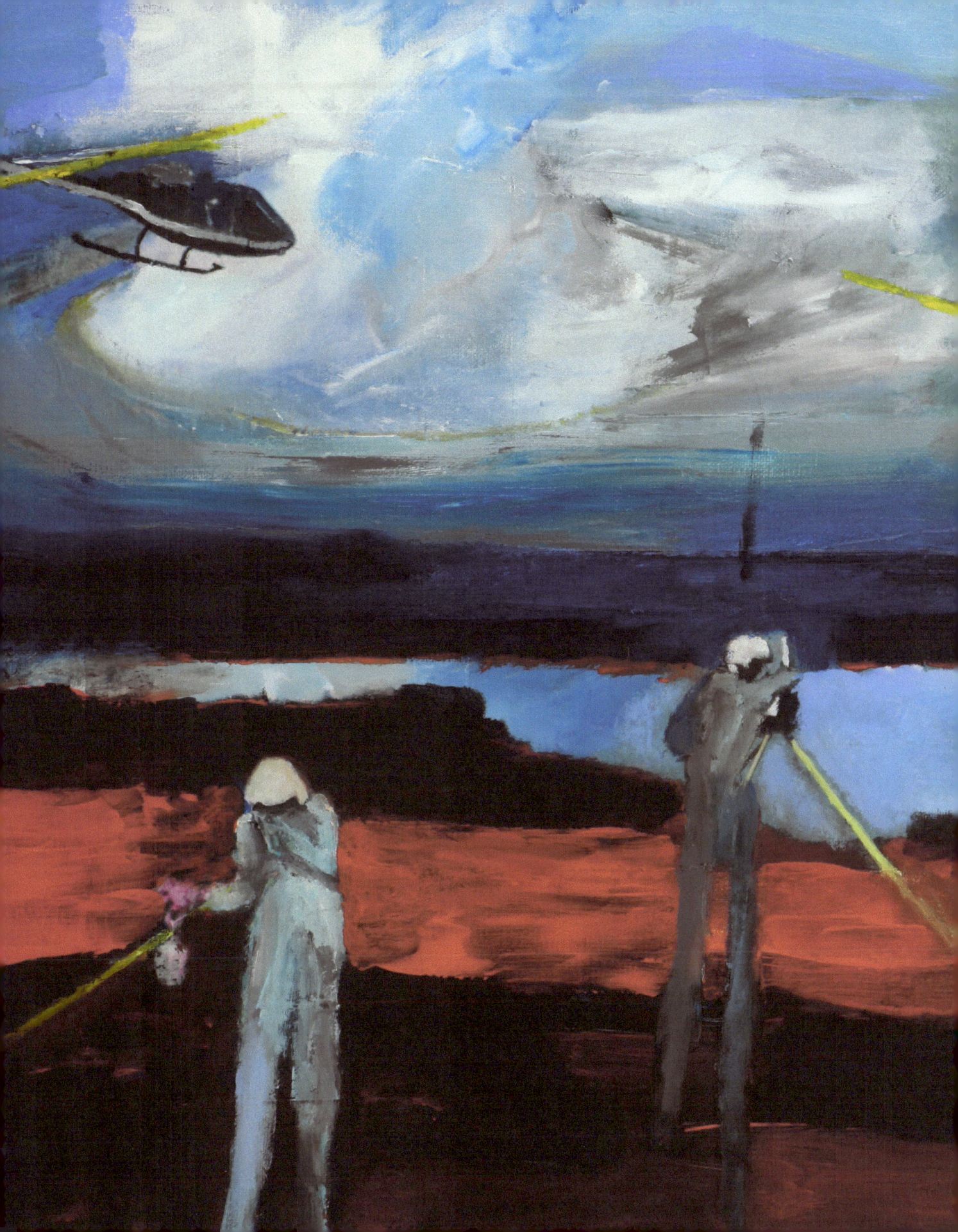

81 | Floods of burning matter

2013
16"x 20"
acrylic paint on canvas

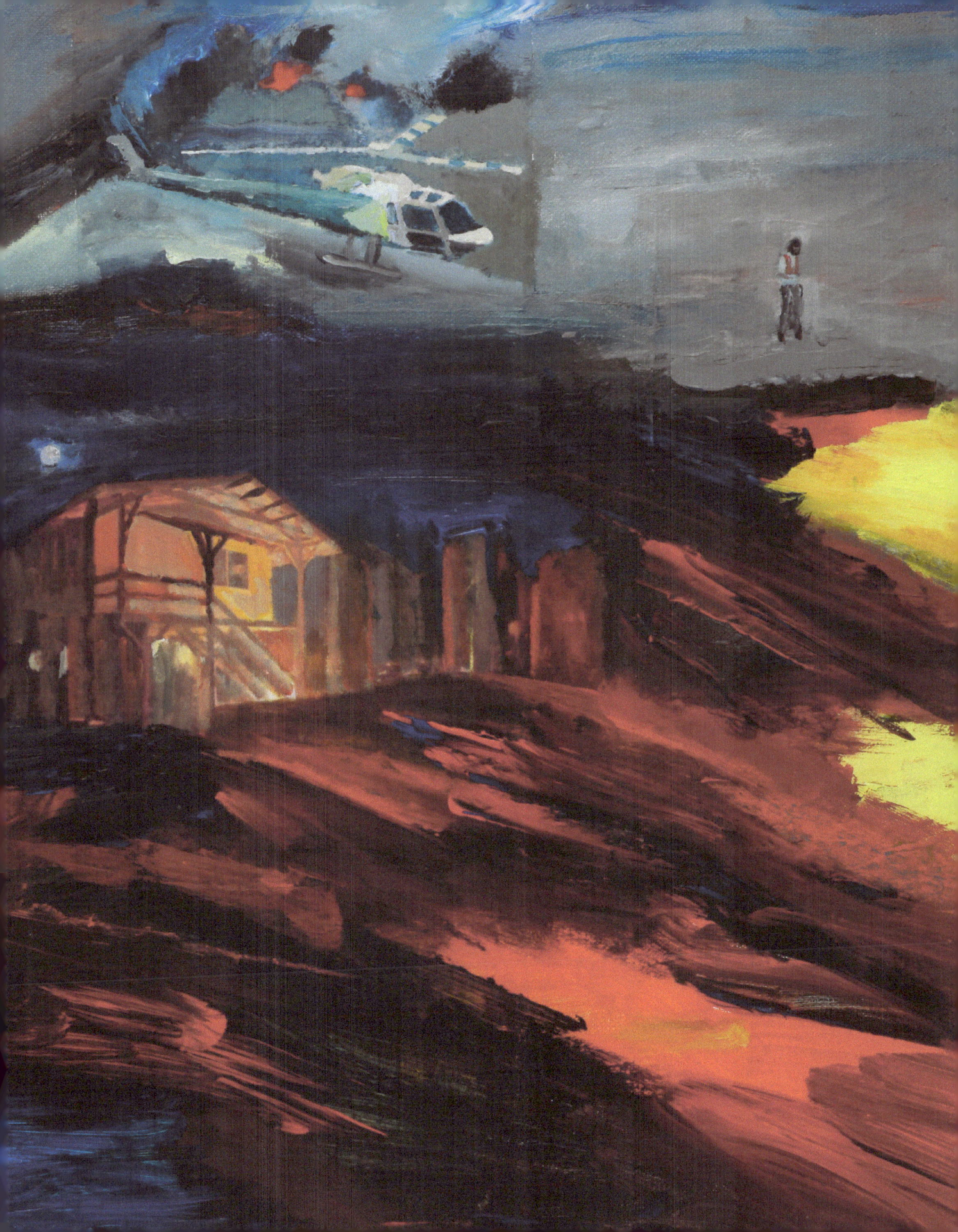

82 | Kīlauea forest figures

2013
16" x 20"
acrylic paint on canvas

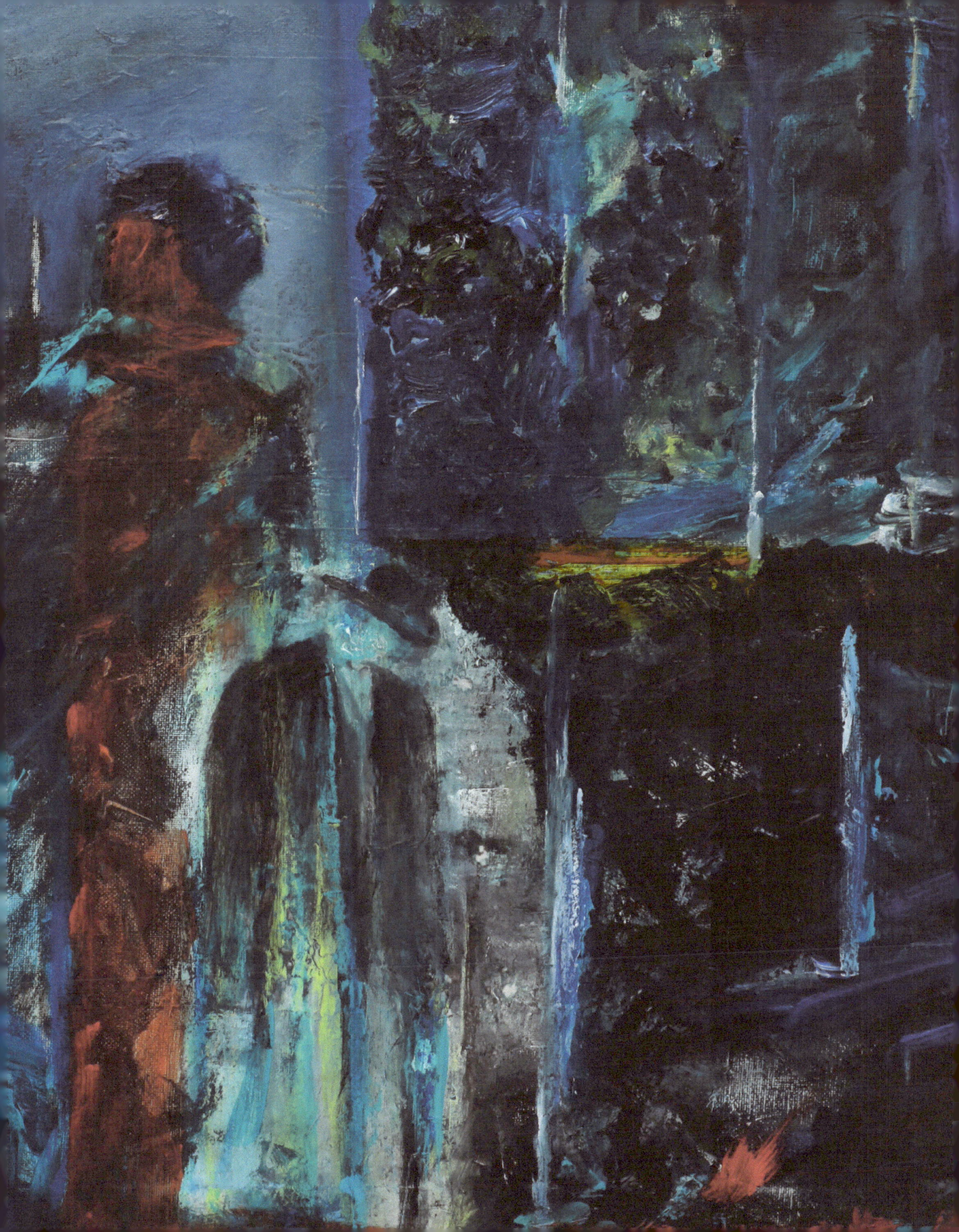

2013
16"x 20"
acrylic paint on canvas

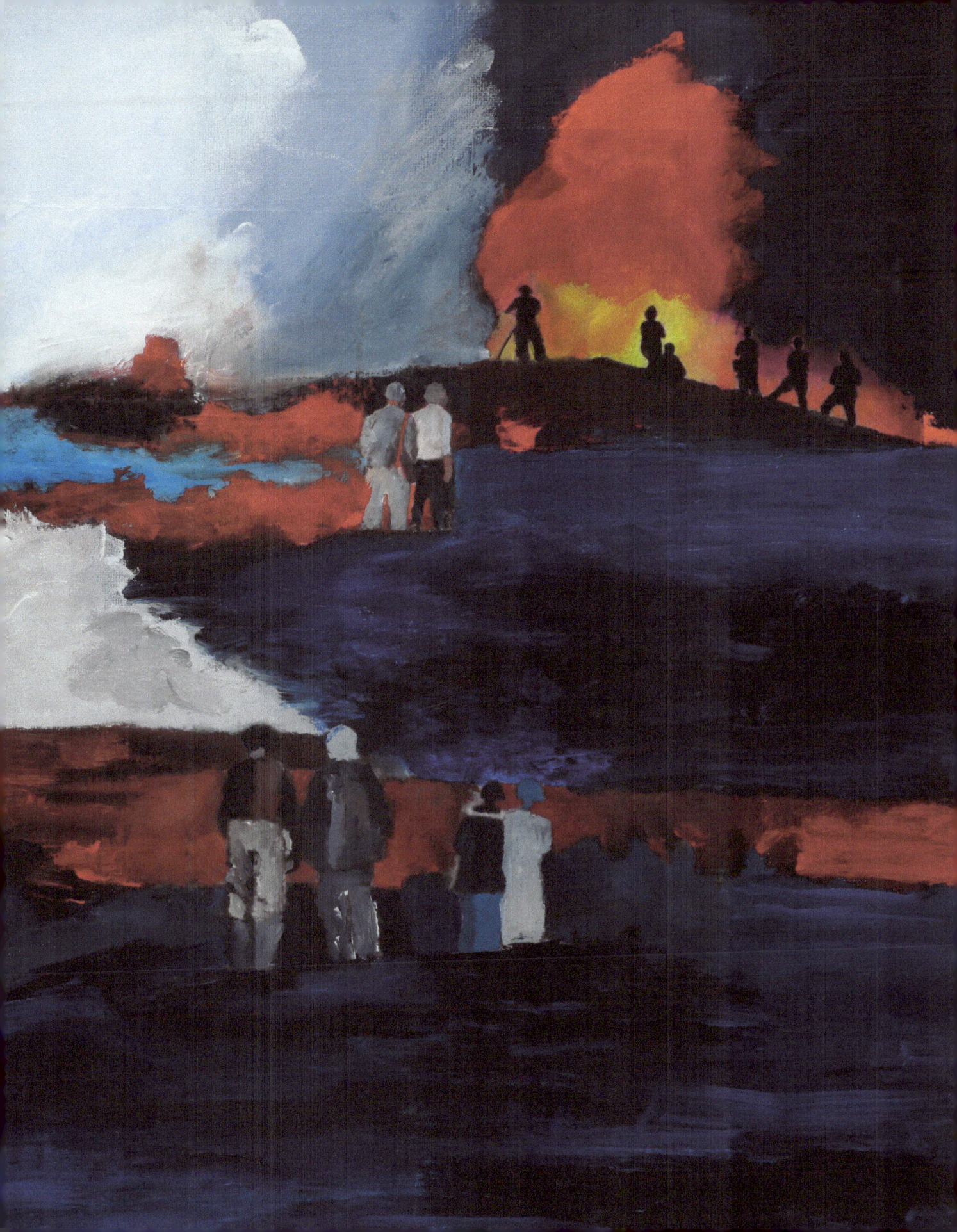

84 | Three Kīlauea observers

2013
16"x 20"
acrylic paint on canvas

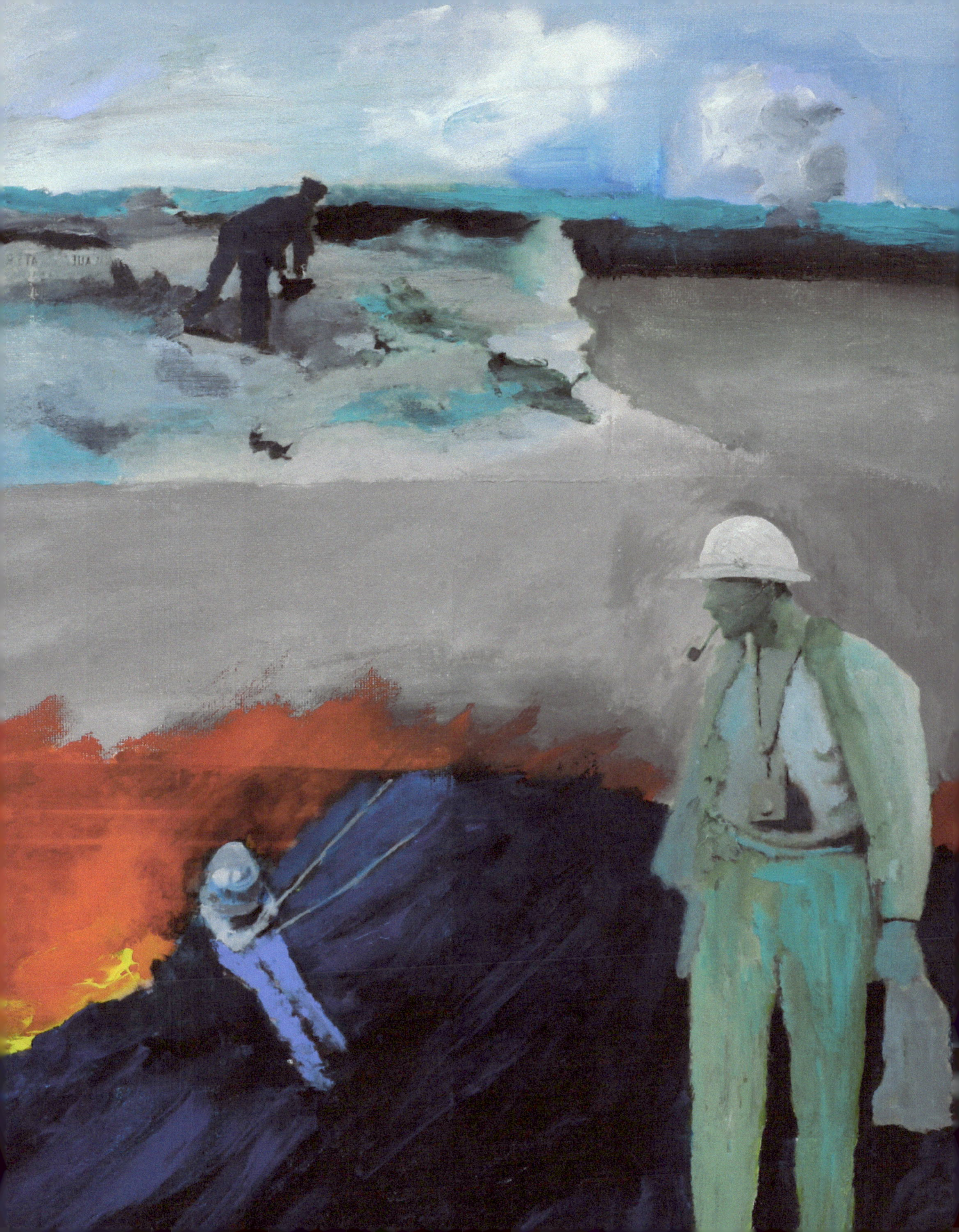

Kīlauea's man-made structures

2013
16"x 20"
acrylic paint on canvas

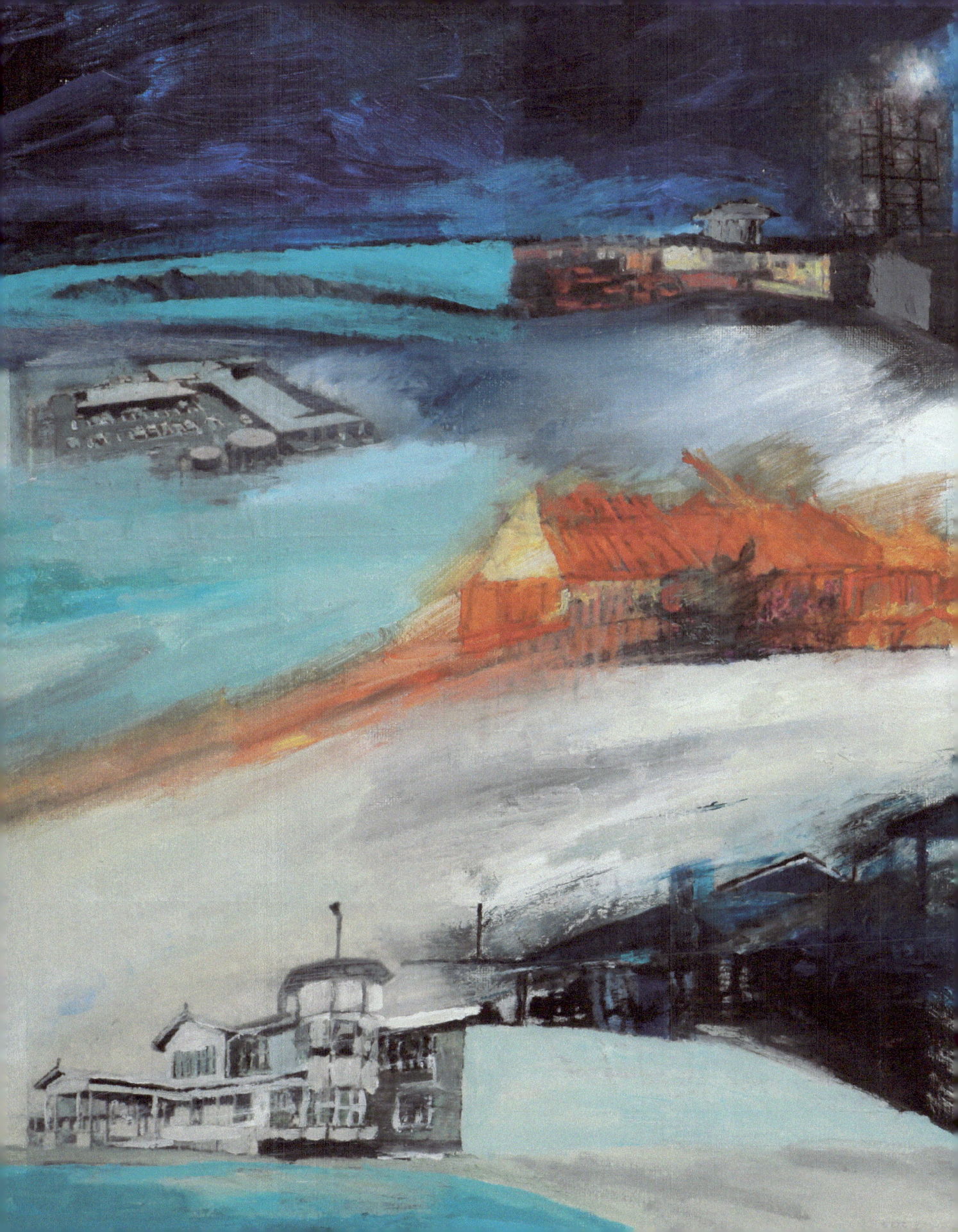

Working above and below water line

2013
16"x 20"
acrylic paint on canvas

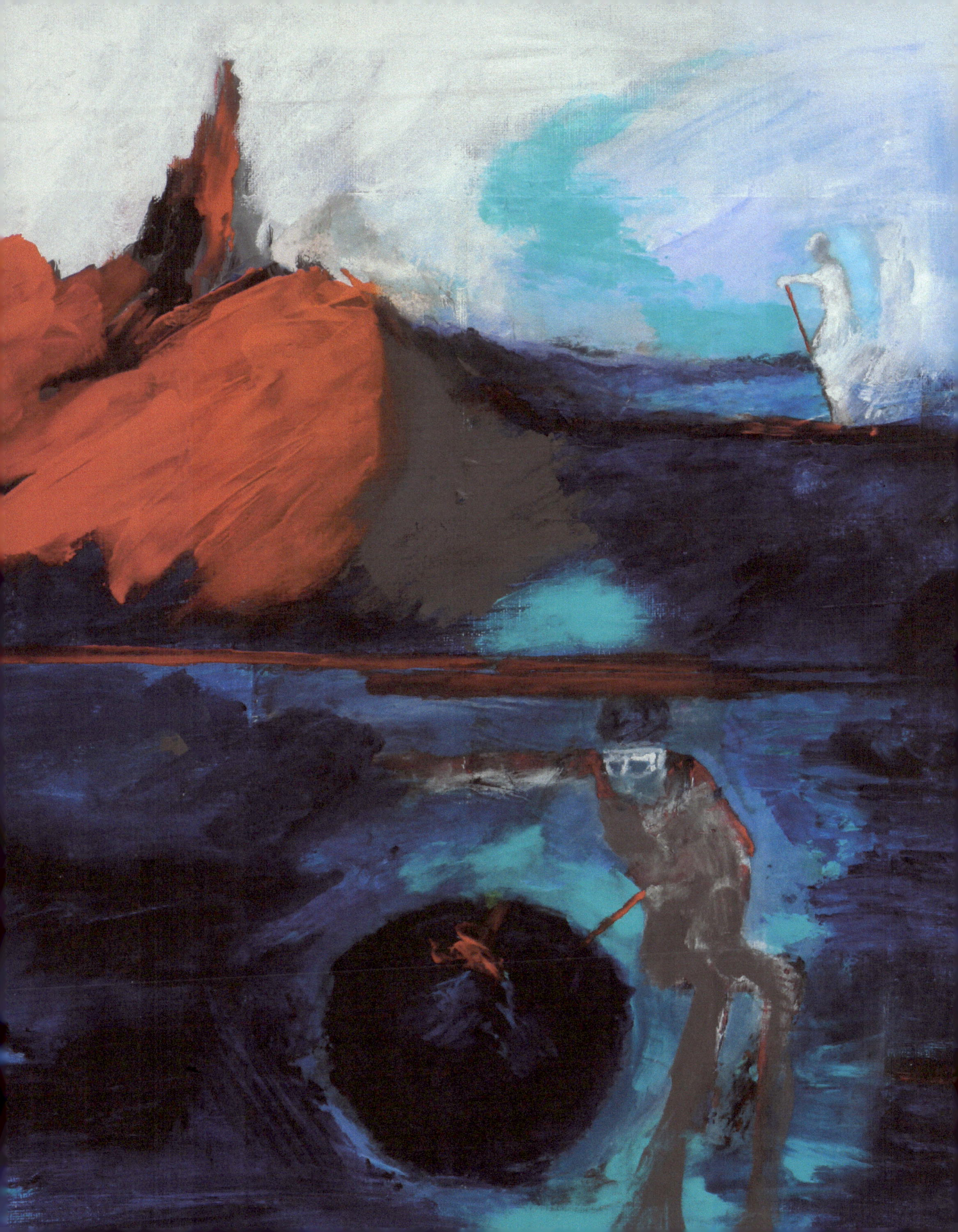

| Monitoring eruption

2013
16"x 20"
acrylic paint on canvas

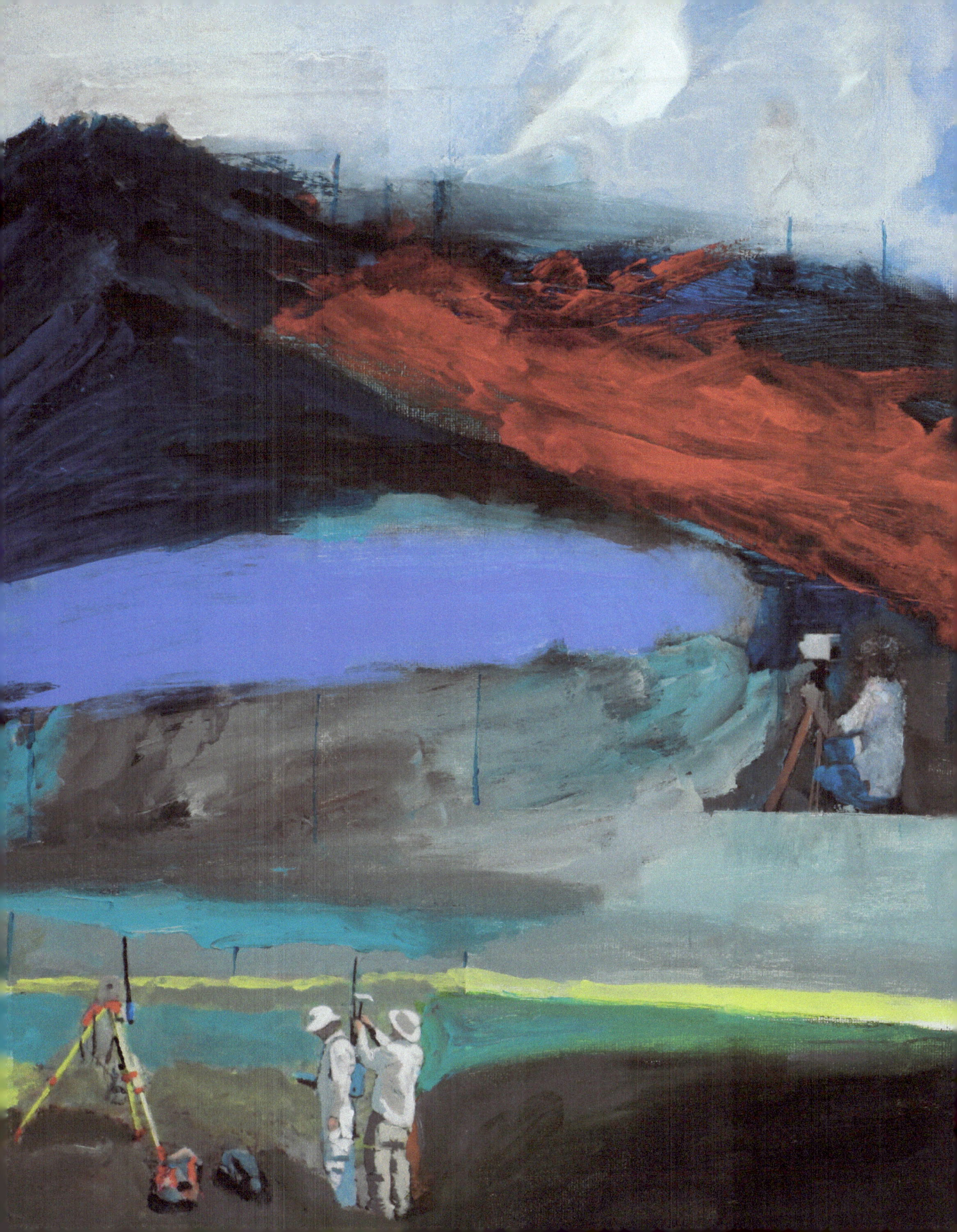

88 | Nēnē crossing

2013
16" x 20"
acrylic paint on canvas

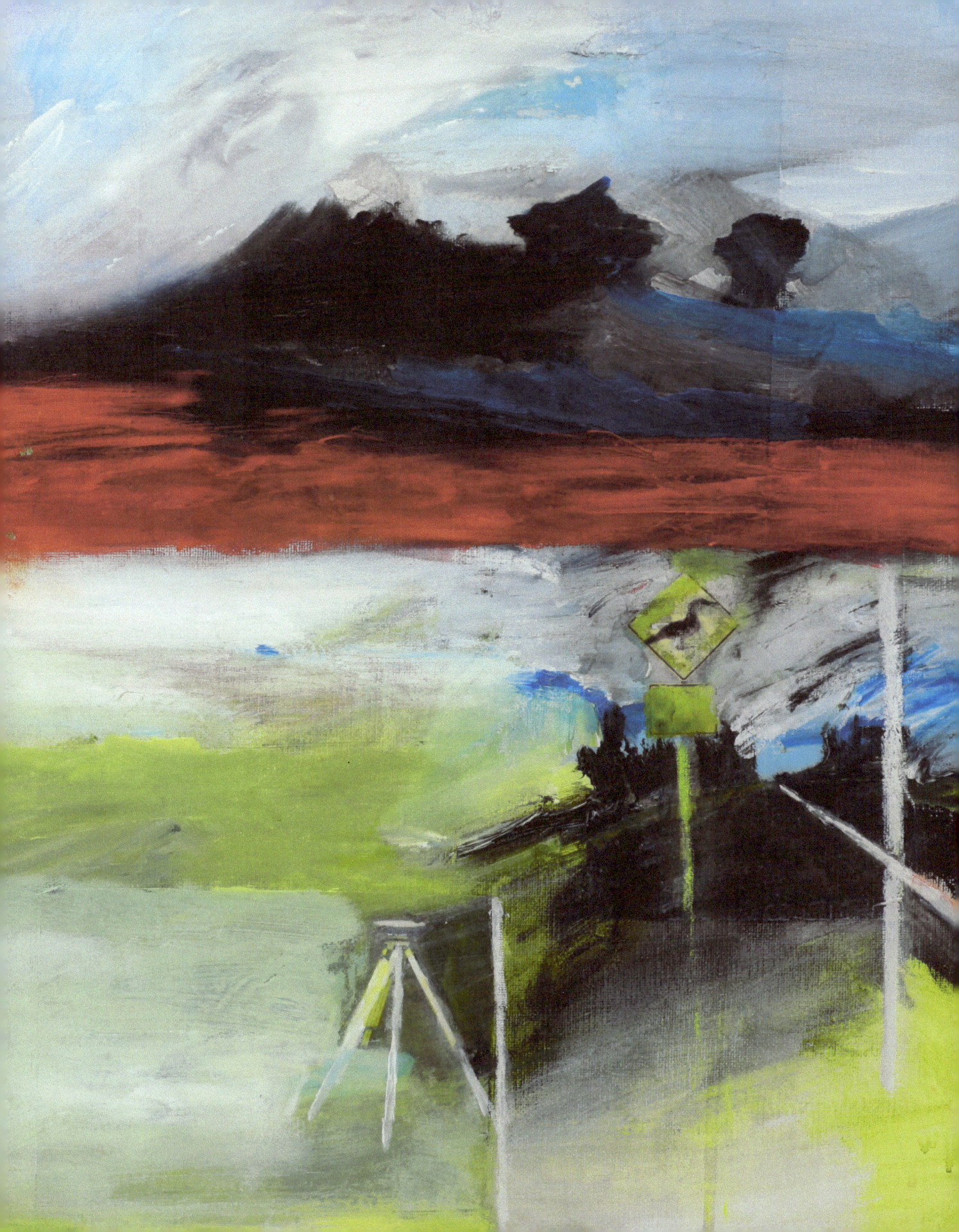

2013
16"x 20"
acrylic paint on canvas

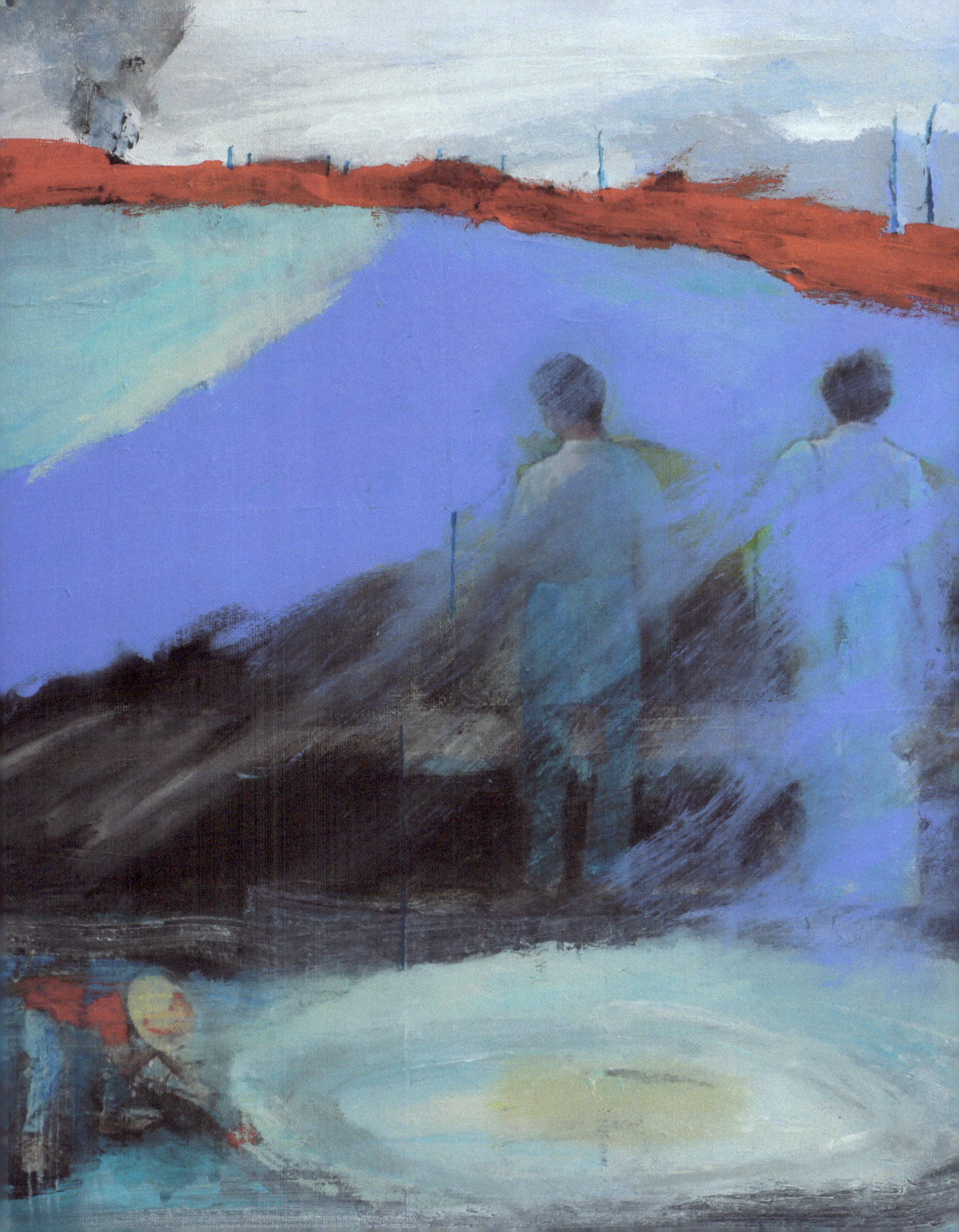

| Red bird with Kīlauea blues

2013
16" x 20"
acrylic paint on canvas

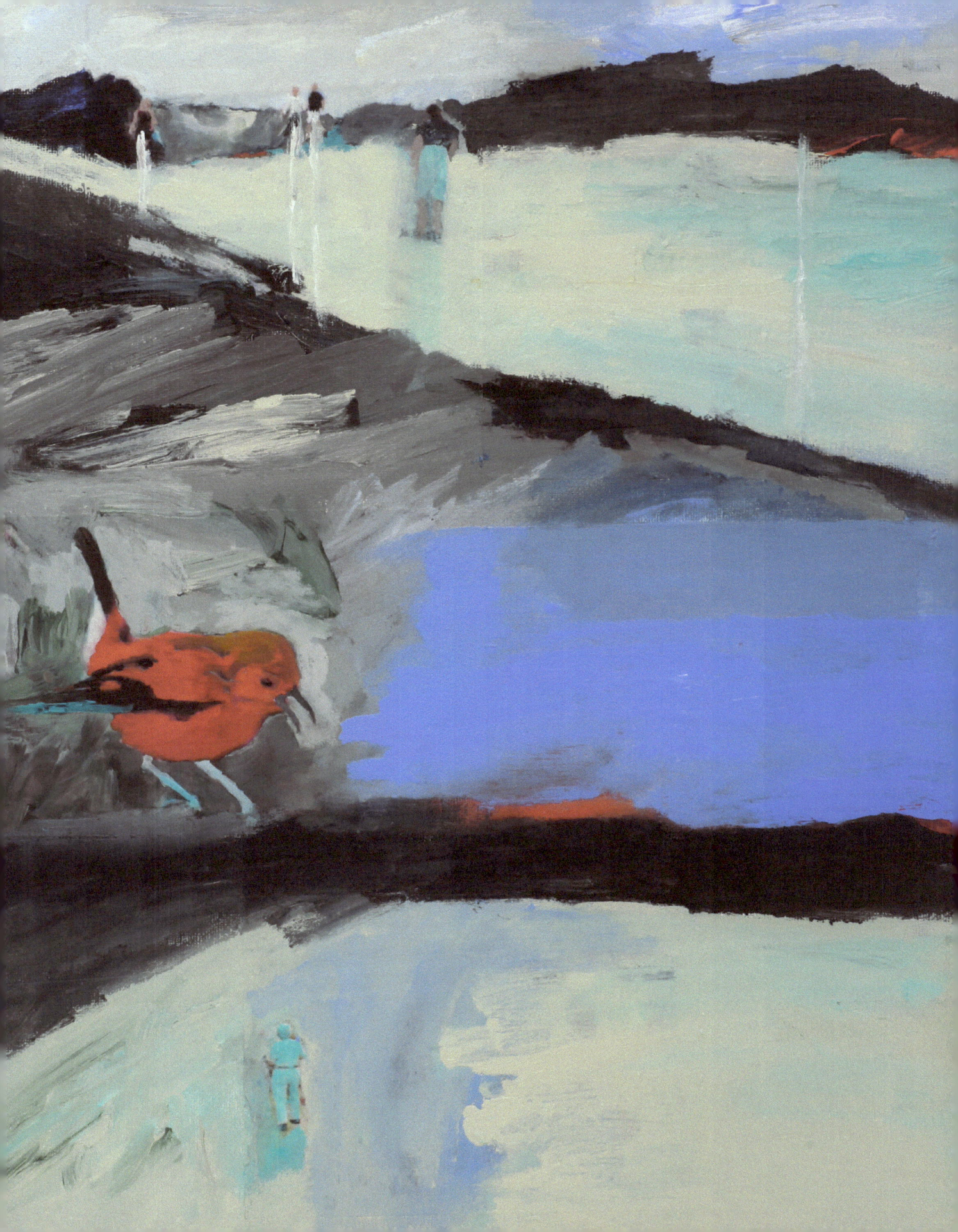

| In the field

2013
16"x 20"
acrylic paint on canvas

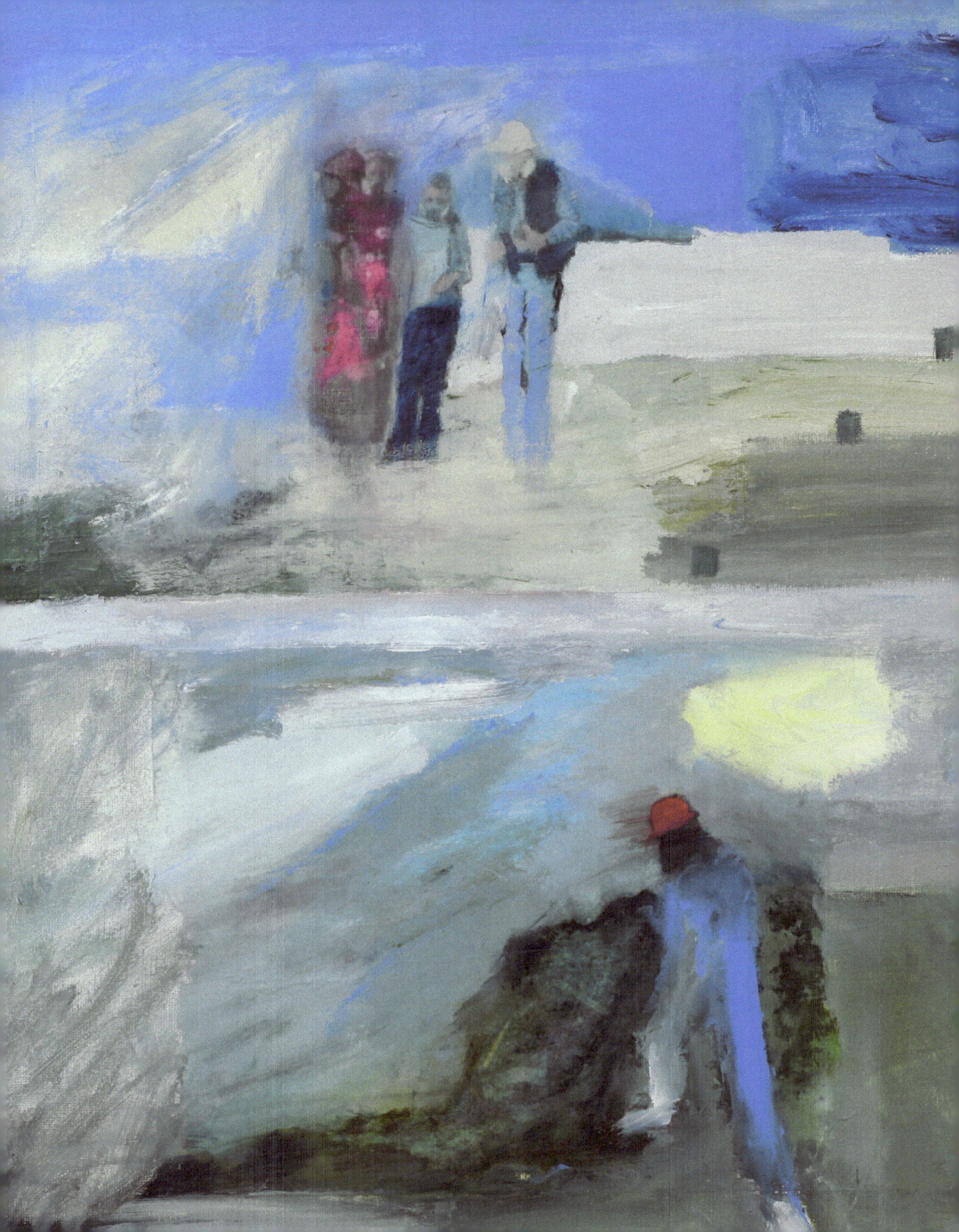

| Finding shade on Kīlauea

2013
16"x 20"
acrylic paint on canvas

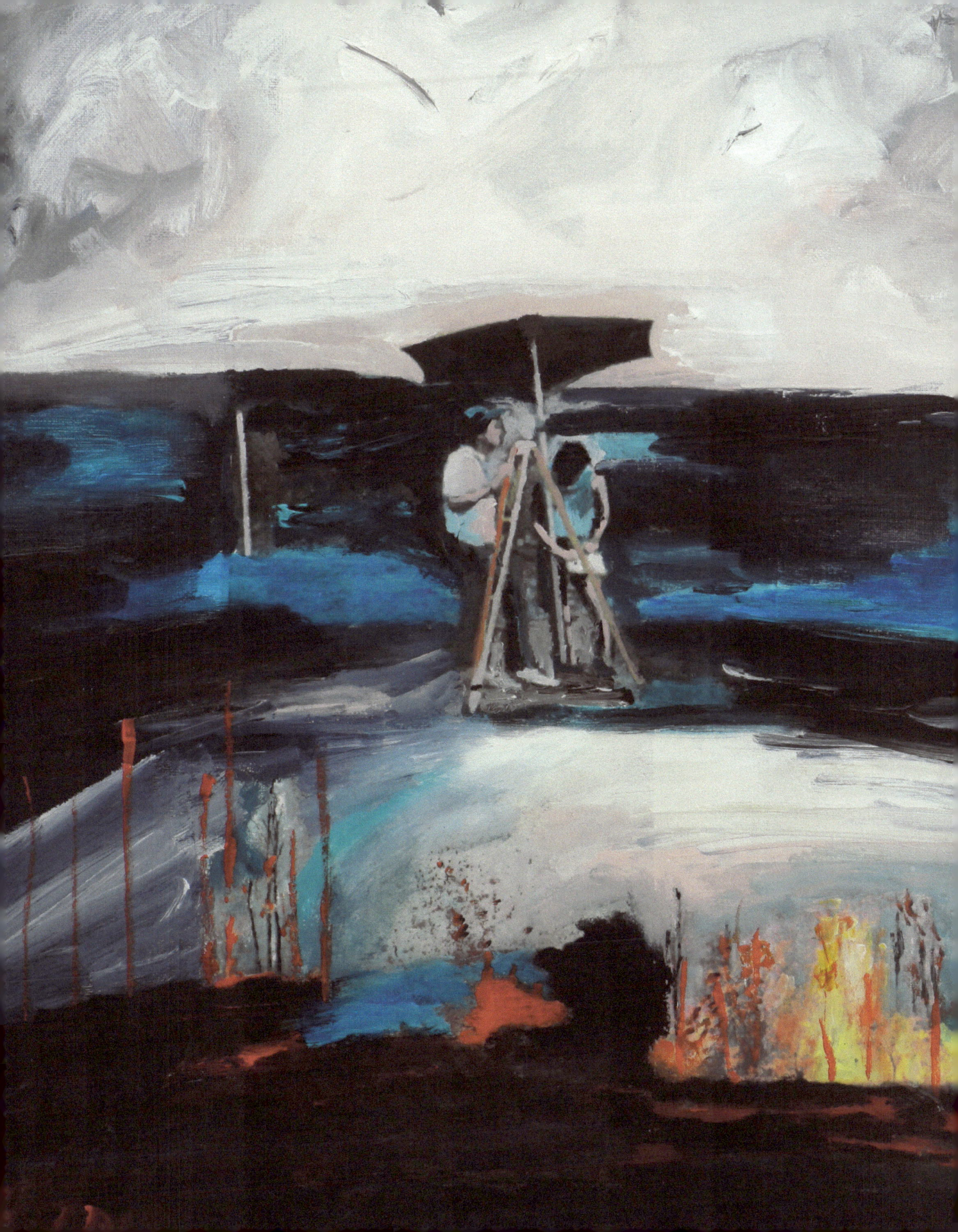

2013
16"x 20"
acrylic paint on canvas

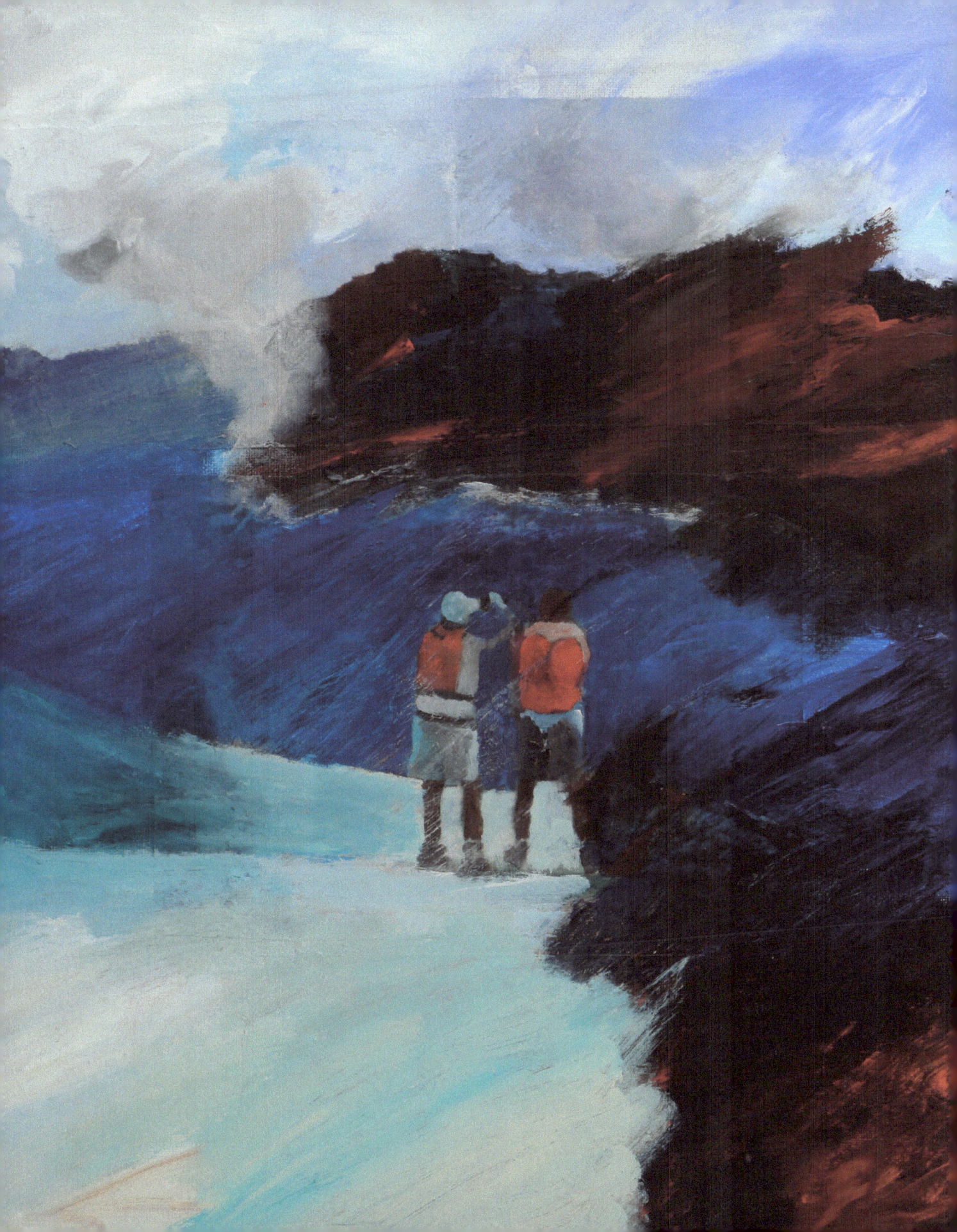

Red splash zone

2013
16" x 20"
acrylic paint on canvas

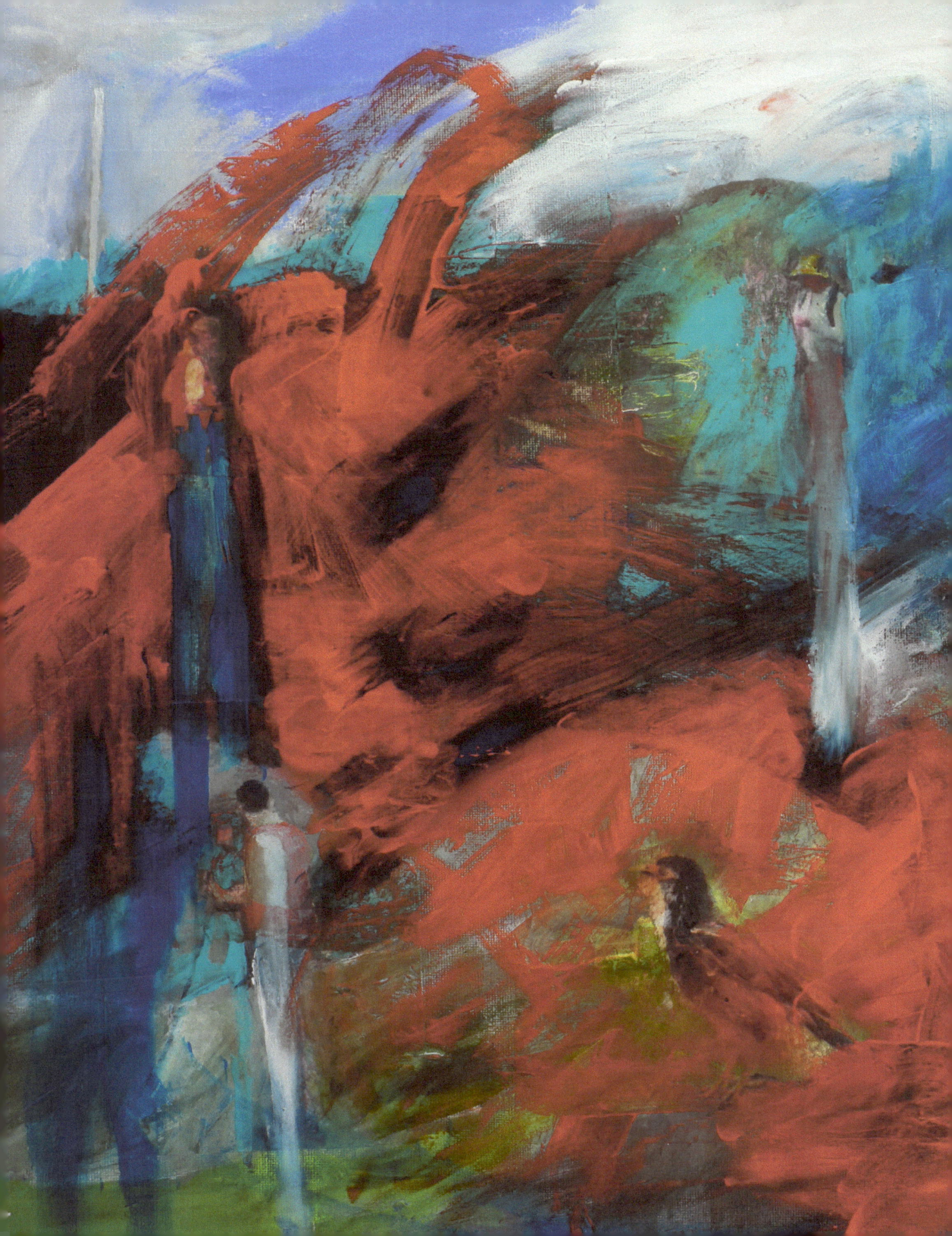

95 | Sunday in the park

2013
16"x 20"
acrylic paint on canvas

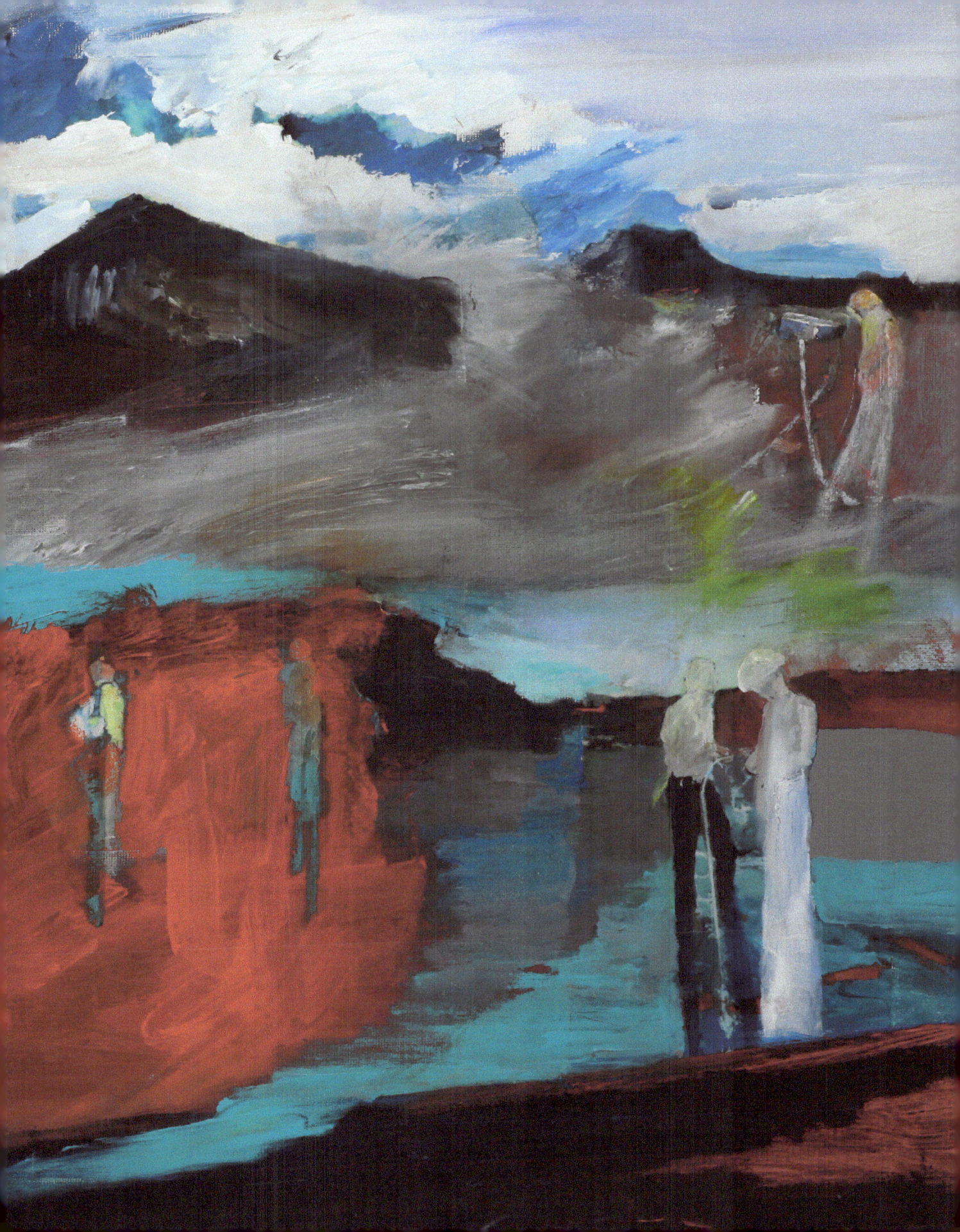

| Sampling Kīlauea

2013
16"x 20"
acrylic paint on canvas

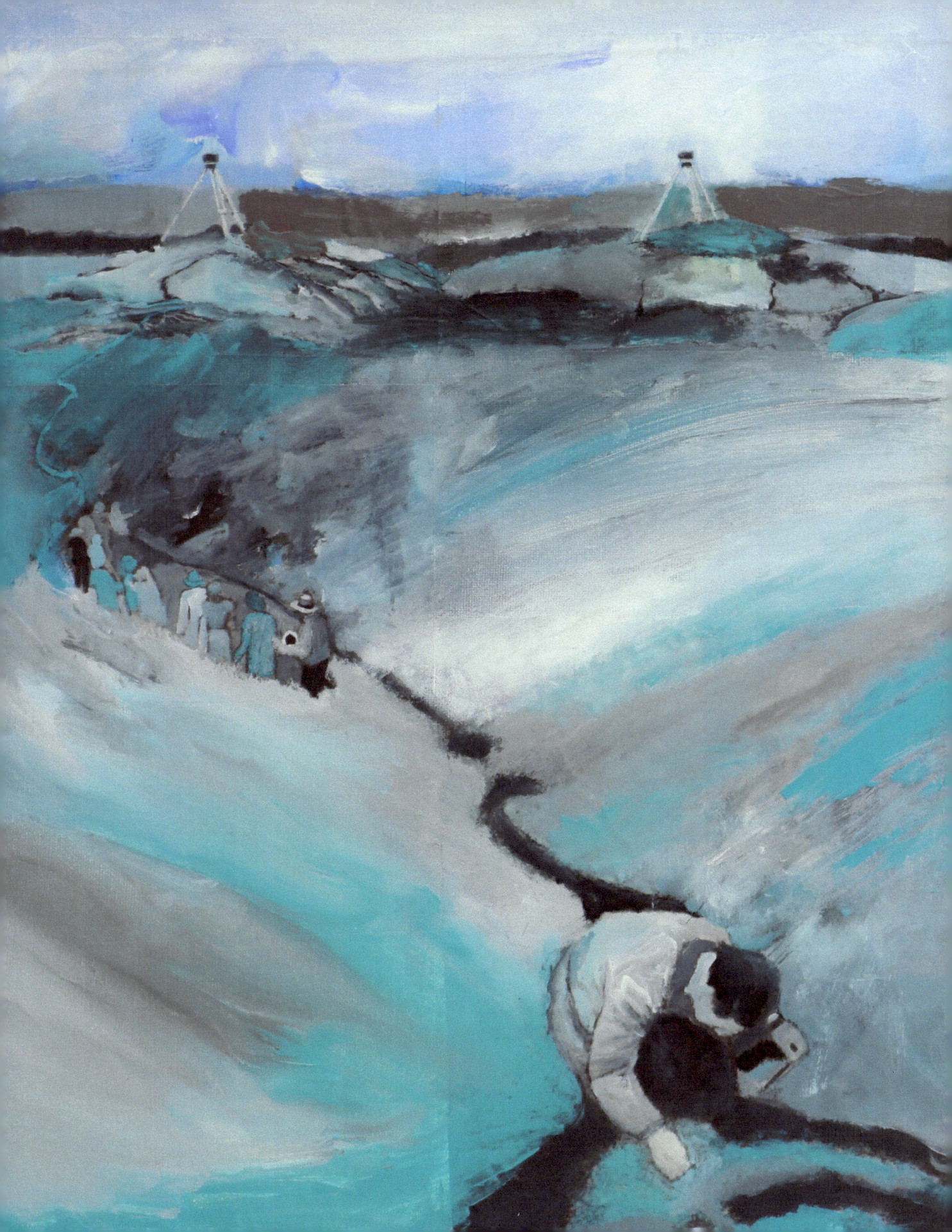

| Clouds, plumes, and vog

2013
16"x 20"
acrylic paint on canvas

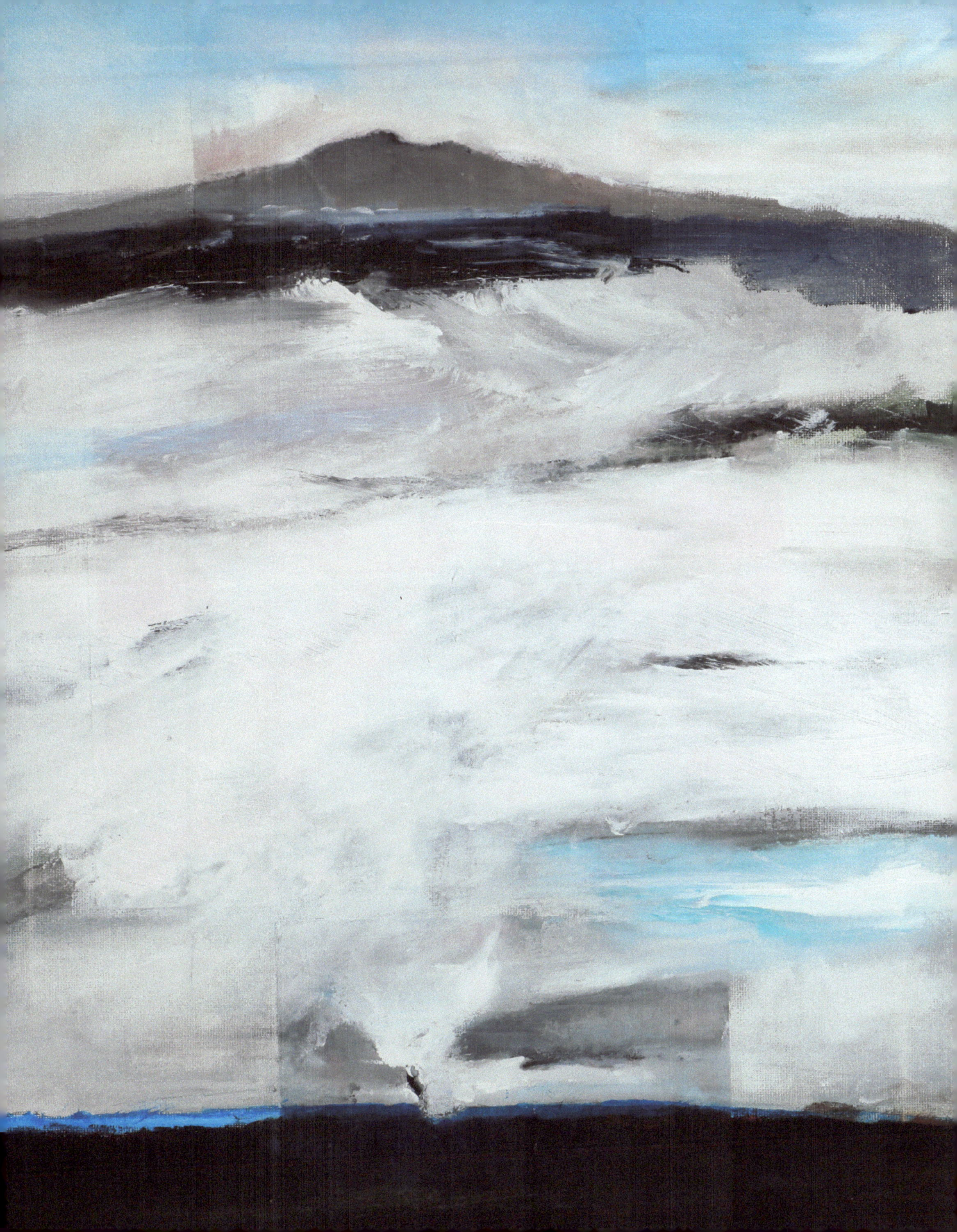

98 | Ocean and crater plumes

2013
16"x 20"
acrylic paint on canvas

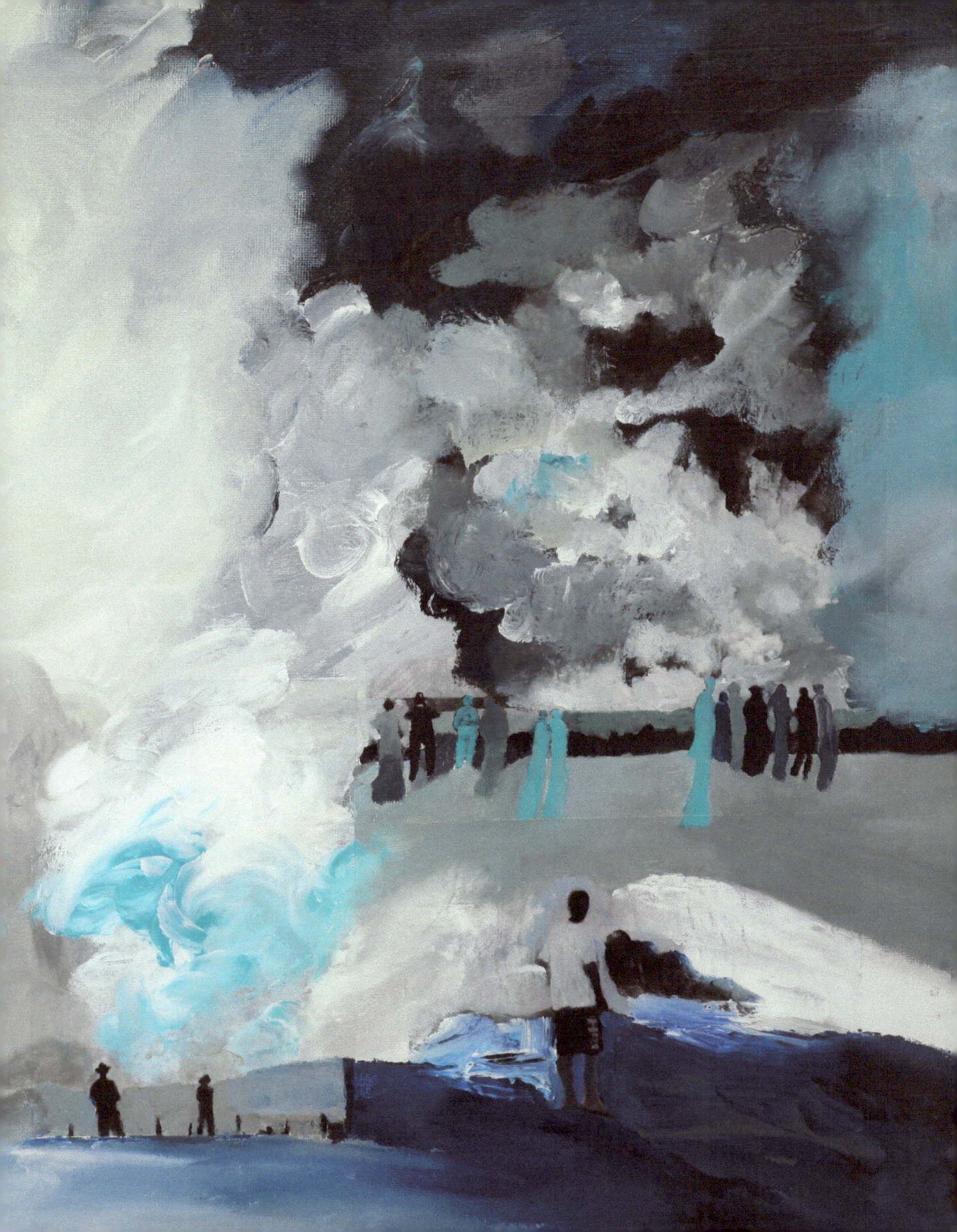

| Roadside geology

2013
16" x 20"
acrylic paint on canvas

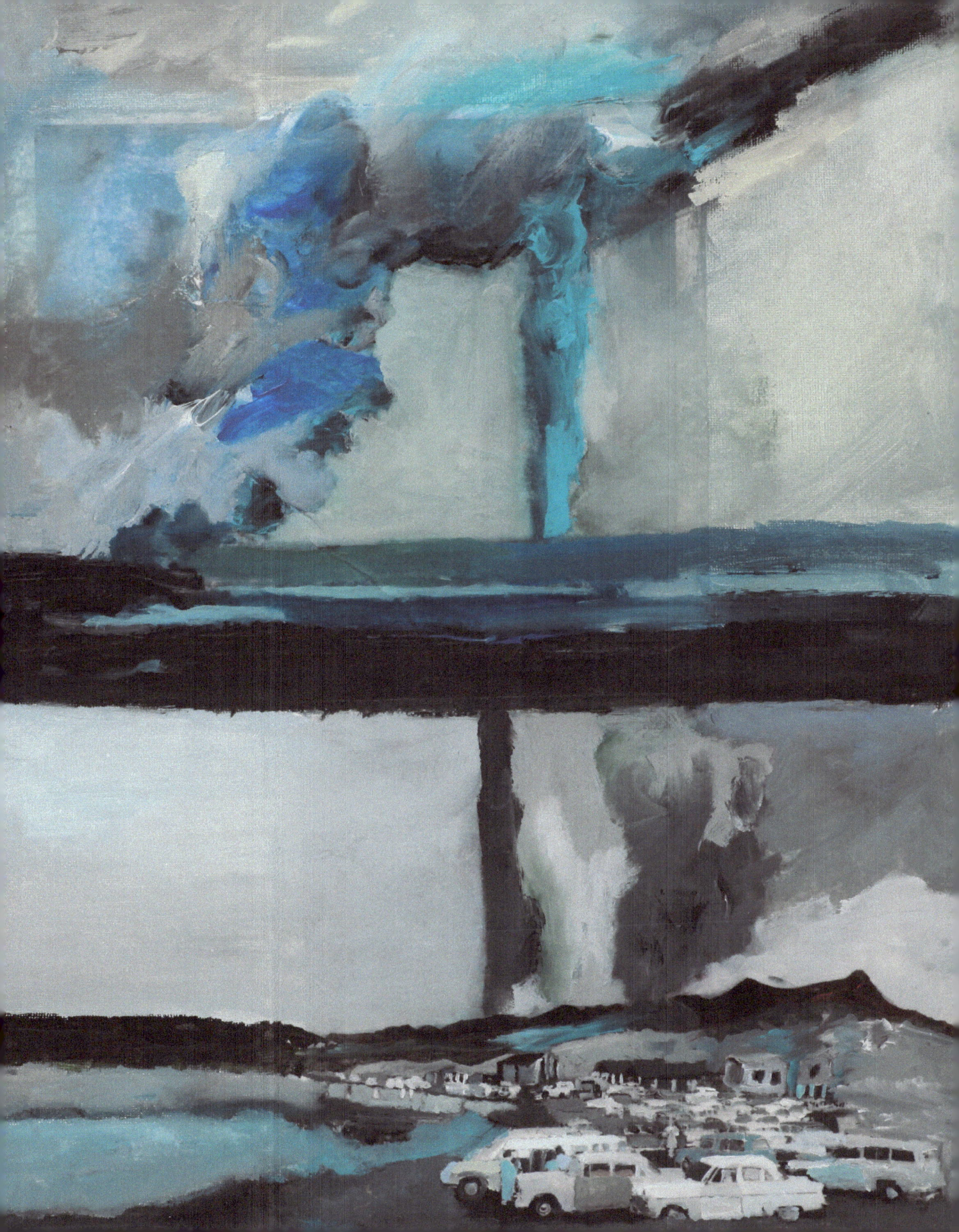

| Black noddy and ʻōmaʻo

2013
16" x 20"
acrylic paint on canvas

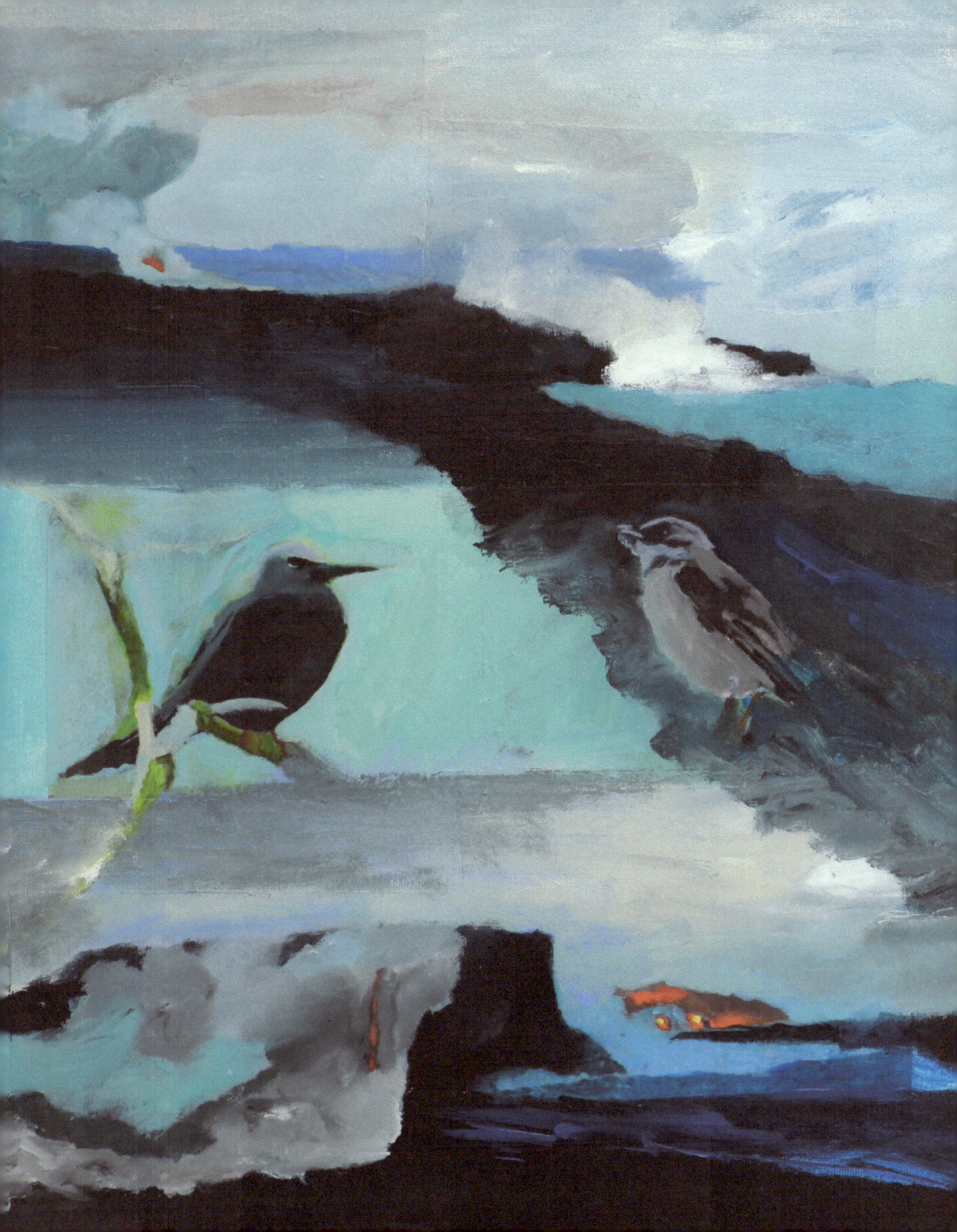

Helen Chellin

For the past 16 years I have lived part time on the Big Island of Hawai'i. Kīlauea Volcano brought me to this island, and I have spent many years hiking, walking, and painting Kīlauea.

I love the shapes, colors and textures of Kīlauea. I love the scale and power of her. She has the ability, like artists, to create, destroy and transform. I love her lava flows and the continual process of change resulting from her eruptions. My paintings utilize multi-layers of images. They combine the viscosity, tactile quality, and hot nature of paint, like lava, with the coolness of photographs. The painted landscapes show changes caused by geology and human intervention.

It is the connection between landscapes and culture that inspires my painting. I paint the scientists who work in the field studying volcanoes. I incorporate the people who live on and who visit Kīlauea's slopes.

I have chosen to paint 100 views of Kīlauea Volcano in honor of one of my mentor artists--Hokusai. Hokusai created the famous work *100 Views of Mt. Fuji.* He was known for being one of the first artists to combine landscape with scenes of people living and working on the flanks of a volcano. My book is dedicated to him and to Christina Heliker, geologist, and photographer, and geologist Margaret T. Mangan. Thirteen years ago I founded the Red Cinder Creativity Center on the Big Island of Hawai'i and was the director of this artist-in-residency program until it closed in 2012.

At the Cité International in Paris and the de Young Museum in San Francisco, I was an artist-in-residence. I also received a State of California Arts Council grant as a teaching artist. In 2008 I created "Tsunami: the Great Wave of Plastic Pollution." This was a science and art installation and performance at the Army Corp of Engineers Bay Model in Sausalito, California. I also had a one person show titled "Toxic Beauty" at 455 Market Street in San Francisco using marine debris plastics collected at South Point in Hawai'i.
In 2009 my work about volcanoes was shown at a USGS Open House in Menlo Park in an exhibit called "The Art in Science" as well as at Harvard University in an exhibit titled "Runaway Nature."
The first fifty paintings in this series of 100 were exhibited at the Wailoa Arts and Cultural Center in Hilo, Hawai'i in October 2013. My artwork is included in many private collections.

You can view more of my artwork at www.helenchellin.com

www.ingramcontent.com/pod-product-compliance
Lightning Source LLC
Chambersburg PA
CBHW050726180526
45159CB00003B/1143

9 780988 887503